John Buchan

THE BATTLE OF THE SOMME:
THE FIRST AND SECOND PHASE

ENDEAVOUR PRESS ⚙

TABLE OF CONTENTS

CHAPTER ONE – PRELIMINARIES

From Arras southward the Western battle-front leaves the coalpits and sour fields of the Artois and enters the pleasant region of Picardy. The great crook of the upper Somme and the tributary vale of the Ancre intersect a rolling tableland, dotted with little towns and furrowed by a hundred shallow chalk streams. Nowhere does the land rise higher than 500 feet, but a trivial swell — such is the nature of the landscape — may carry the eye for thirty miles. There are few detached farms, for it is a country of peasant cultivators who cluster in villages. Not a hedge breaks the long roll of cornlands, and till the higher ground is reached the lines of tall poplars flanking the great Roman highroads are the chief landmarks.

At the lift of country between Somme and Ancre copses patch the slopes, and sometimes a church spire is seen above the trees from some woodland hamlet. The Somme winds in a broad valley between chalk bluffs, faithfully dogged by a canal — a curious river which strains, like the Oxus, "through matted rushy isles," and is sometimes a lake and sometimes an expanse of swamp. The Ancre is such a stream as may be found in Wiltshire, with good trout in its pools. On a hot midsummer day the slopes are ablaze with yellow mustard, red poppies and blue cornflowers; and to one coming from the lush flats of Flanders, or the "black country" of the Pas de Calais, or the dreary levels of Champagne, or the strange melancholy Verdun hills, this land wears a habitable and cheerful air, as if remote from the oppression of war.

The district is known as the Santerre. Some derive the name from *sana terra* — the healthy land; others from *sarta terra* — the cleared land. Some say it is *sancta terra*, for Peter the Hermit was a Picard, and the piety of the Crusaders enriched the place with a thousand relics and a hundred noble churches. But there are those — and they have much to say for themselves — who read the name *sang terre* — the bloody land, for the Picard was the Gascon of the north, and the countryside is an old cockpit of war. It was the seat of the government of Clovis and Charlemagne. It was ravaged by the Normans, and time and again by the English. There Louis XI and Charles the Bold fought their battles; it suffered terribly in the Hundred Years'

War; German and Spaniard, the pandours of Eugene and the Cossacks of Alexander marched across its fields; from the walls of Peronne the last shot was fired in the war of 1814. And in the greatest war of all it was destined to be the theatre of a struggle compared with which its ancient conflicts were like the brawls of a village fair.

Till Midsummer in 1916 the Picardy front had shown little activity. Since that feverish September when de Castelnau had extended on the Allies' left, and Maud'huy beyond de Castelnau, in the great race for the North Sea, there had been no serious action. Just before the Battle of Verdun began the Germans made a feint south of the Somme and gained some ground at Frise and Dompierre.

There had been local raids and local bombardments, but the trenches on both sides were good, and a partial advance offered few attractions to either. Amiens was miles behind one front, vital points like St. Quentin and Courtrai and La Fère were far behind the other. In that region only a very great and continuous offensive would offer any strategic results. In September, 1915, the British took over most of the line from Arras to the Somme, and on the whole they had a quiet winter in their new trenches. This long stagnation led to one result: it enabled the industrious Germans to excavate the chalk hills on which they lay into a fortress which they believed to be impregnable. Their position was naturally strong, and they strengthened it by every device which science could provide. Their High Command might look uneasily at the Aubers ridge and Lens and Vimy, but they had no doubts about the Albert heights.

*

The German plan in the West, after the first offensive had been checked at the Marne and Ypres, was to hold their front with abundant guns but the bare minimum of men, and use their surplus forces to win a decision in the East. This scheme was foiled by the heroic steadfastness of Russia's retreat, which surrendered territory freely but kept her armies in being.

During the winter of 1915-16 the German High Command were growing anxious. They saw that their march to the Dvina and their adventure in the Balkans had wholly failed to shake the resolution of their opponents. They were aware that the Allies had learned with some exactness the lesson of eighteen months of war, and that even now they were superior in men, and would presently be on an equality in ammunition. Moreover, the Allied command was becoming concentrated and shaking itself free from its old passion for divergent operations. Our generals had learned the wisdom of the order of the King of Syria to his captains: "Fight neither with small nor great but only with the King of Israel"; and the King of Israel did not welcome the prospect.

Now, to quote a famous saying of General Foch, "A weakening force must always be attacking," and from the beginning of 1916 the Central Powers were forced into a continuous offensive. Their economic strength was draining rapidly. Their people had been told that victory was already won, and were asking what had become of the fruits of it. They feared greatly the coming Allied offensive, for they knew that it would be simultaneous on all fronts, and they cast about for a means of frustrating it.

That was the reason of the great Verdun assault. Germany hoped, with the obtuseness that has always marked her estimate of other races, so to weaken the field strength of France that no future blow would be possible and the French nation, weary and dispirited, would incline to peace. She hoped, in any event, to lure the Allies into a premature counter-attack, so that their great offensive might go off at half-cock and be defeated piece-meal.

None of these things happened. Pétain at Verdun handled the defence like a master. With a wise parsimony he refused to use up any unit. When a division had suffered it was taken out of the line and replaced by a fresh one, so that none of the *cadres* were destroyed. He was willing enough to yield ground, if only the enemy paid his price. His aim was not to hold territory, for he knew well that he would some day regain with interest all he had surrendered, but to destroy the German field army. His plan succeeded.

The German force was, as the French say, *accroché* at Verdun, and was compelled to go on long after any hope of true success had vanished. The place became a trap where Germany was bleeding to death. Meanwhile, with the full assent of General Joffre, the Generalissimo in the West, the British armies made no movement. They were biding their time.

Early in June the ill-conceived Austrian attack on the Trentino had been checked by Italy, and suddenly — in the East — Russia swung forward to a surprising victory. Within a month nearly half a million Austrians had been put out of action, and the distressed armies of the Dual Monarchy called on Germany for help.

The inevitable von Hindenburg was brought into play, and such divisions as could be spared were despatched from the West. At this moment, when the grip was tightening in the East, France and Britain made ready for the supreme effort of the war.

Germany's situation was intricate and uneasy. She had no large surplus of men immediately available at her interior depots. The wounded who were ready again for the line and the young recruits from the 1917 class were all needed to fill up the normal wastage in her ranks. She had no longer any great mass of strategic reserves. Most had been sucked into the maelstrom of Verdun or despatched East to von Hindenburg. At the best, she had a certain number of divisions which represented a local and temporary surplus in some particular area.

Beyond these she could only get reinforcements by the process known as "milking the line" — taking out a battalion here and a battalion there — an expedient both cumbrous and wasteful, for these battalions were not fresh troops, and their removal was bound to leave many parts of her front perilously thin. Germany in the West was holding a huge salient — from the North Sea to Soissons, and from Soissons to Verdun. If a wedge were driven in on one side the whole apex would be in deadly danger. The Russian field army could retire safely from Warsaw and Vilna, because it was mobile and lightly equipped, but an army which had been stationary for eighteen months and had relied mainly upon its fortifications would be apt to find a Sedan in any retirement. The very strength of the German front in the West constituted its weakness. A breach in a fluid line may be mended, but a breach in a rigid and most intricate front cannot be filled unless there are large numbers of men available for the task or unlimited time. We have seen that there were no such numbers, and it was likely that the Allies would see that there was no superfluity of leisure.

The path of wisdom for Germany in June was undoubtedly to fall back in good order to a much shortened line, which with her numbers might be strongly held. There is reason to believe that soon after the beginning of the Allied bombardment some such policy was considered. The infantry commanders of the 17th Corps were warned to be prepared for long marches and heavy rearguard fighting, instructions were given for holding bridgeheads far in the rear, and officers were advised that the retreat might be either a retirement at ease or a withdrawal under pressure from the enemy. Had such a course been taken it would have been unfortunate for the Allied plans. But such a course was impossible. The foolish glorification after the naval battle of May '81 forbade it. The German people had been buoyed up under the discomfort of the British blockade by tales of decisive successes in the field. The German Chancellor had almost tearfully implored his enemies to look at the map, to consider the extent of German territorial gains, and to admit that they were beaten. He was one of those who did not fulfil Foch's definition of military wisdom.

"The true soldier is the man who ignores that science of geographical points which is alien to war, which is the negation of war and the sure proof of decadence, the man who knows and follows one vital purpose — to smash the enemy's field force."

The dancing dervishes of Pan-Germanism had already announced in detail the use to which the occupied territories would be put. For Germany to fall back from the Somme to the Meuse would have toppled down the whole flimsy edifice of German confidence. It was unthinkable; her political commitments were too great; her earlier vainglory sat like an Old Man of the Sea on her shoulders.

Yet, in spite of this weakness in the strategic situation, the German stronghold in the West was still formidable in the extreme. From Arras southward they held in the main the higher ground. The front consisted of a strong first position, with firing, support, and reserve trenches and a labyrinth of deep dug-outs; a less strong intermediate line covering the field batteries; and a second position some distance behind, which was of much the same strength as the first. Behind lay fortified woods and villages which could be readily linked up with trench lines to form third and fourth positions. The attached trench map will give some idea of the amazing complexity of the German defences. They were well served by the great network of railways which radiate from La Fère and Laon, Cambrai, and St. Quentin, and many new light lines had been constructed.

They had ample artillery and the use to which the occupied territories would be put. For Germany to fall back from the Somme to the Meuse would have toppled down the whole flimsy edifice of German confidence. It was unthinkable; her political commitments were too great; her earlier vainglory sat like an Old Man of the Sea on her shoulders.

Yet, in spite of this weakness in the strategic situation, the German stronghold in the West was still formidable in the extreme. From Arras southward they held in the main the higher ground. The front consisted of a strong first position, with firing, support, and reserve trenches and a labyrinth of deep dug-outs; a less strong intermediate line covering the field batteries; and a second position some distance behind, which was of much the same strength as the first. Behind lay fortified woods and villages which could be readily linked up with trench lines to form third and fourth positions. The attached trench map will give some idea of the amazing complexity of the German defences. They were well served by the' great network of railways which radiate from La Fère and Laon, Cambrai, and St. Quentin, and many new light lines had been constructed. They had ample artillery and shells, endless machine-guns, and consummate skill in using them.

It was a fortress to which no front except the West could show a parallel. In the East the line was patchy and not continuous. The Russian soldiers who in the early summer were brought to France stared with amazement at a ramification of trenches compared with which the lines in Poland and Galicia were like hurried improvisations.

*

The British Armies had in less than two years grown from the six divisions of the old Expeditionary Force to a total of some seventy divisions in the field, leaving out of account the troops supplied by the Dominions and by India.

Behind these divisions were masses of trained men to replace wastage for at least another year. With the possible exception of France, Great Britain had mobilised for the direct and indirect purposes of war a larger proportion of her population than any other belligerent country. Moreover while engaged in also supplying her Allies, she had provided this vast levy with all its necessary equipment.

Britain is so fond of decrying her own efforts that few people have realised the magnitude of her achievement. There is no precedent for it in the history of the world. She jettisoned all her previous theories and calculations; and in a society which had not for a hundred years been called upon to make a great effort against an enemy, a society highly differentiated and industrialised, a society which lived by sea-borne commerce and so could not concentrate like certain other lands exclusively on military preparation, she provided an army on the largest scale, and provided it out of next to nothing. She had to improvise officers and staff, auxiliary services, munitionment — everything. She had to do this in the face of an enemy already fully prepared. She had to do it, above all, at a time when war had become a desperately technical and scientific business and improvisation was most difficult. It is easy enough to assemble quickly hordes of spearmen and pikemen, but it would seem impossible to improvise men to use the bayonet and machine gun, the bomb and the rifle. But Britain did it — and did it for the most part by voluntary enlistment.

The quality of the result was not less remarkable than the quantity. The efficiency of the supply and transport, the medical services, the aircraft work, was universally admitted. Our staff and intelligence work — most difficult to improvise — was now equal to the best in the field. Our gunnery was praised by the French, a nation of expert gunners. As for the troops themselves we had secured a homogeneous army of which it was hard to say that one part was better than the other. The original Expeditionary Force — the "Old Contemptibles," who for their size were probably the best body of fighting men on earth — had mostly disappeared. Territorial battalions were present at the First Battle of Ypres, and New Service battalions at Hooge and Loos.

By June, 1916, the term New Armies was a misnomer. The whole British force in one sense was new. The famous old regiments of the line had been completely renewed since Mons, and their drafts were drawn from the same source as the men of the new battalions. The only difference was that in the historic battalions there was a tradition already existing, whereas in the new battalions that tradition had to be created. And the creation was quick. If the Old Army bore the brunt of the First Battle of Ypres, the Territorials were no less heroic in the Second Battle of Ypres, and the New Army had to its credit the four-mile charge at Loos. It was no patchwork force which in June was drawn up in Picardy, but the flower of the manhood of the British Empire, differing in origin and antecedents, but alike in discipline and courage and resolution.

Munitions had grown with the numbers of men. Anyone who was present at Ypres in April and May, 1915, saw the German guns all day pounding our lines with only a feeble and intermittent reply. It was better at Loos in September, when we showed that we could achieve an intense bombardment. But at that date our equipment sufficed only for spasmodic efforts and not for that sustained and continuous fire which was needed to destroy the enemy's defences. Things were very different in June, 1916. Everywhere on the long British front there were British guns — heavy guns of all calibres, field guns innumerable, and in the trenches there were quantities of trench-mortars. The great munition dumps, constantly depleted and constantly replenished from distant bases, showed that there was food and to spare for this mass of artillery, and in the factories and depots at home every minute saw the reserves growing. Britain was manufacturing and issuing weekly as much as the whole stock of land service ammunition which she possessed at the outbreak of war. The production of high explosives was sixty-six times what it had been at the beginning of 1915. The monthly output of heavy guns had been multiplied by six in the past year, and that of machine-guns by fourteen. We no longer fought against a far superior machine. We had created our own machine to nullify the enemy's and allow our manpower to come to grips.

*

About the middle of June on the whole ninety-mile front held by the British, and on the French front north and south of the Somme there began an intermittent bombardment of the German lines.

There were raids at different places, partly to mislead the enemy as to the real point of assault, and partly to identify the German units opposed to us. Such raids varied widely in method, but they were extraordinarily successful. Sometimes gas was used, but more often after a short bombardment a picked detachment crossed no-man's-land, cut the enemy's wire, and dragged home a score or two of prisoners.

One, conducted by a company of the Highland Light Infantry near the Vermelles-La Bassée Road, deserves special mention.

Our guns had damaged the German parapets, so when darkness came a German working-party was put in to mend them. The Scots, while the engineers neatly cut off a section of German trenches, swooped down on the place, investigated the dug-outs, killed two score Germans, brought back forty-six prisoners, and had for total casualties two men slightly wounded. During these days, too, there were many fights in the air.

It was essential to prevent German airplanes from

crossing our front and observing our preparations. Our own machines scouted far into the enemy hinterland, reconnoitring and destroying.

On Sunday, June 25th, the bombardment became intenser. It fell everywhere on the front; German trenches were obliterated at Ypres and Arras as well as at Beaumont Hamel and Fricourt. There is nothing harder to measure than the relative force of such a "preparation," but had a dispassionate observer been seated in the clouds he would have noted that from Gommecourt to a mile or two south of the Somme the Allied fire was especially methodical and persistent. On Wednesday, June 28th, from an artillery observation post in that region it seemed as if a complete devastation had been achieved. Some things like broken telegraph poles were all that remained of what, a week before, had been leafy copses. Villages had become heaps of rubble. Travelling at night on the roads behind the front — from Bethune to Amiens — the whole eastern sky was lit up with what seemed fitful summer lightning. But there was curiously little noise. In Amiens, a score or so of miles from the firing line, the guns were rarely heard, whereas fifty miles from Ypres they sound like a roll of drums and wake a man in the night. The configuration of that part of Picardy muffles sound, and the country folk call it the Silent Land.

All the last week of June the weather was grey and cloudy, with a thick brume on the uplands, which made air-work unsatisfactory. There were flying showers of rain and the roads were deep in mire. At the front — through the haze — the guns flashed incessantly, and there was that tense expectancy which precedes a great battle. Troops were everywhere on the move, and the shifting of ammunition dumps nearer to the firing-line foretold what was coming. There was a curious exhilaration everywhere. Men felt that this at last was the great offensive, that this was no flash in the pan, but a movement conceived on the grand scale as to guns and men which would not cease until a decision was reached. But, as the hours passed in mist and wet, it seemed as if the fates were unpropitious. Then, on the last afternoon of June, there came a sudden change. The pall of cloud cleared away and all Picardy swam in the translucent blue of a summer evening. That night the orders went out. The attack was to be delivered next morning three hours after dawn.

The first day of July dawned hot and cloudless, though a thin fog, the relic of the damp of the past week, clung to the hollows. At half-past five the hill just west of Albert offered a singular view. It was almost in the centre of the section allotted to the Allied attack, and from it the eye could range on the left up and beyond the Ancre glen to the high ground around Beaumont Hamel and Serre; in front to the great lift of tableland beyond which lay Bapaume; and to the right past the woods of Fricourt to the valley of the Somme. All the slopes to the east were wreathed in smoke, which blew aside now and then and revealed a patch of wood or a church spire. In the foreground lay Albert, the target of an occasional German shell, with its shattered Church of Notre Dame de Bebrières and the famous gilt Virgin hanging head downward from the campanile. All along the Allied front, a couple of miles behind the line, captive balloons, the so-called "sausages," glittered in the sunlight. Every gun on a front of twenty-five miles was speaking, and speaking without pause. In that week's bombardment more light and medium ammunition was expended than the total amount manufactured in Britain during the first eleven months of war, while the heavy stuff produced during the same period would not have kept our guns going for a single day. Great spurts of dust on the slopes showed where a heavy shell had burst, and black and white gouts of smoke dotted the middle distance like the little fires in a French autumn field. Lace-like shrapnel wreaths hung in the sky, melting into the morning haze. The noise was strangely uniform, a steady rumbling, as if the solid earth were muttering in a nightmare, and it was hard to distinguish the deep tones of the heavies, the vicious whip-like crack of the field-guns and the bark of the trench-mortars.

About 7.15 the bombardment rose to that hurricane pitch of fury which betokened its close. Then appeared a marvellous sight, the solid spouting of the enemy slopes — as if they were lines of reefs on which a strong tide was breaking. In such a hell it seemed that no human thing could live. Through the thin summer vapour and the thicker smoke which clung to the foreground there were visions of a countryside actually moving — moving bodily in debris into the air. And now there was a new sound — a series of abrupt and rapid bursts which came gustily from the first lines, like some colossal machine-gun. These were the new trench mortars — those wonderful little engines of death. There was another sound, too, from the North, as if the cannonading had suddenly come nearer. It looked as if the Germans had begun a counter-bombardment on part of the British front line.

The staff officers glanced at their watches, and at half-past seven precisely there came a lull. It lasted for a second or two, and then the guns continued their tale. But the range had been lengthened everywhere, and from a bombardment the fire had become a *barrage*. For, on a twenty-five mile front, the Allied infantry had gone over the parapets.

CHAPTER TWO – THE FIRST STAGE

The point of view of the hill-top was not that of the men in the front trenches. The crossing of the parapets is the supreme moment in modern war. What has been the limit suddenly becomes the starting point. The troops are outside defences, moving across the open to investigate the unknown. It is the culmination of months of training for officers and men, and the least sensitive feels the drama of the crisis. Most of the British troops engaged had twenty months before been employed in peaceable civilian trades. In their ranks were every class and condition — miners from north England, factory hands from the industrial centres, clerks and shop-boys, ploughmen and shepherds, Saxon and Celt, college graduates and dock labourers, men who in the wild places of the earth had often faced danger, and men whose chief adventure had been a Sunday bicycle ride. Nerves may be attuned to the normal risks of trench warfare and yet shrink from the desperate hazard of a charge into the enemy's line.

But to one who visited the front before the attack the most vivid impression was that of quiet cheerfulness. These soldiers of Britain were like Cromwell's Ironsides, they "knew what they fought for and loved what they knew." There were no shirkers and few who wished themselves elsewhere. One man's imagination might be more active than another's, but the will to fight, and to fight desperately, was universal. With the happy gift of the British soldier they had turned the ghastly business of war into something homely and familiar. They found humour in danger and discomfort, and declined to regard the wildest crisis as wholly divorced from their normal life. Accordingly they took everything as part of the day's work, and awaited the supreme moment without heroics and without tremor, confident in themselves, confident in their guns, and confident in the triumph of their cause. There was no savage lust of battle, but that far more formidable thing — a resolution which needed no rhetoric to support it. Norfolk's words were true of every man of them:

> "As gentle and as jocund as to jest
> Go I to fight. Truth hath a quiet breast."

A letter written before the action by a young officer gives noble expression to this joyful resolution. He fell in the first day's battle and the letter was posted after his death:

"*I am writing this letter to you just before going into action to-morrow morning about dawn.*

"*I am about to take part in the biggest battle that has yet been fought in France, and one which ought to help to end the war very quickly.*

"*I never felt more confident or cheerful in my life before, and would not miss the attack for anything on earth. The men are in splendid form, and every officer and man is more happy and cheerful than I have ever seen them. I have just been playing a rag game of football in which the umpire had a revolver and a whistle.*

"*My idea in writing this letter is in case I am one of the 'costs,' and get killed. I do not expect to be, but such things have happened, and are always possible.*

"*It is impossible to fear death out here when one is no longer an individual, but a member of a regiment and of an army. To be killed means nothing to me, and it is only you who suffer for it; you really pay the cost.*

"*I have been looking at the stars, and thinking what an immense distance they are away. What an insignificant thing the loss of, say, 40 years of life is compared with them! It seems scarcely worth talking about.*

"Well, good-bye, you darlings. Try not to worry about it, and remember that we shall meet again really quite soon.

"This letter is going to be posted if...Lots of love. From your loving son,

"Qui procul hinc
Ante diem periit,
Sed miles, sed pro Patria."

The British aim in this, the opening stage of the battle, was the German first position. The attached map shows its general line. In the section of assault, running from north to south, it covered Gommecourt, passed east of Hebuterne, followed the high ground in front of Serre and Beaumont Hamel, and crossed the Ancre a little to the northwest of Thiepval. It ran in front of Thiepval, which was very strongly fortified, east of Authuille, and just covered the hamlets of Ovillers and La Boisselle. There it ran about a mile and a quarter east of Albert. It then passed south round the woodland village of Fricourt, where it turned at right angles to the east, covering Mametz and Montauban. Half-way between Maricourt and Hardecourt it turned south again, covered Curlu, crossed the Somme at the wide marsh near the place called Vaux, covered Frise and Dompierre and Soyecourt, and passed just east of Lihons, where it left the sector with which we are now concerned. The position was held by the right wing of the 2nd Army (formerly von Buelow's, but now under von Below, a brother of the General commanding on the extreme left in Poland), and the troops in line opposite the British on July 1st were principally the 14th Reserve Corps, made up of Baden, Wurtemberg and Bavarian divisions.

*

It is clear that the Germans expected the attack of the Allies and had made a fairly accurate guess as to its *terrain*. They assumed that the area would be from Arras to Albert. In all that area they were ready with a full concentration of men and guns. South of Albert they were less prepared, and south of the Somme they were caught napping. The history of the first day is therefore the story of two separate actions in the north and south, in the first of which the Allies failed and in the second of which they brilliantly succeeded. By the evening the first action had definitely closed, and the weight of the Allies was flung wholly into the second.

That is almost inevitable in an attack on a very broad front. Some part will be found tougher than the rest, and that part having been tried will be relinquished; but it is the stubbornness of the knot and the failure to take it which are the price of success elsewhere. Let us first tell the tale of the desperate struggle between Gommecourt and Thiepval.

The divisions in action there were mainly from the New Army, though there were two of the old regulars, which had won fame both in Flanders and Gallipoli. They had to face a chain of fortified villages — Gommecourt, Serre, Beaumont Hamel, and Thiepval — and enemy positions which were generally on higher and better ground. The Ancre cut the line in two, with steep slopes rising from the valley bottom. Each village had been so fortified as to be almost impregnable, with a maze of catacombs, often two storeys deep, where whole battalions could take refuge, underground passages from the firing line to sheltered places in the rear, and pits into which machine guns could be lowered during a bombardment. On the plateau behind, with excellent direct observation, the Germans had their guns massed.

It was this direct observation and the deep shelters for machine-guns which were the undoing of the

British attack from Gommecourt to Thiepval. As our bombardment grew more intense on the morning of July 1st, so did the enemy's. Before our men could go over the parapets the Germans had plastered our front trenches with high explosives and in many places blotted them out. All along our line, fifty yards before and behind the first trench, they dropped 6-in. and 8-in. high explosive shells. The result was that our men instead of forming up in the front trench were compelled to form up in the open ground behind, for the front trench had disappeared. In addition to this there was an intense shrapnel *barrage* which must have been directed by observers, for it followed our troops as they moved forward.

At Beaumont Hamel we had constructed a mine, the largest known in the campaign. At 7.30 acres of land leaped into the air, and our men advanced under the shadow of a pall of dust which turned the morning into twilight. "The exploding chamber," said a sergeant, describing it afterwards, "was as big as a picture palace, and the gallery was an awful length. It took us seven months to build, and we were working under some of the crack Lancashire miners. Every time a fresh fatigue party came up they'd say to the miners, 'Ain't your etceteraed grotto ever going up?'

But, my lord! it went up all right on July 1st. It was the sight of your life. Half the village got a rise. The air was full of stuff — waggons, wheels, horses, tins, boxes and Germans. It was seven months well spent getting that mine ready. I believe some of the pieces are coming down still."

As we began to cross no-man's-land, the Germans seemed to man their ruined parapets, and fired rapidly with automatic rifles and machine-guns. They had special light *mousqueton* battalions, armed only with machine-guns, who showed marvellous intrepidity, some even pushing their guns forward into no-man's-land to enfilade our advance.

The British moved forward in line after line, dressed as if on parade; not a man wavered or broke rank; but minute by minute the ordered lines melted away under the deluge of high-explosive, shrapnel, rifle and machine-gun fire. There was no question about the German weight of artillery.

From dawn till long after noon they maintained this steady drenching fire. Gallant individuals or isolated detachments managed here and there to break into the enemy position, and some even penetrated well behind it, but these were episodes, and the ground they won could not be held. By the evening, from Gommecourt to Thiepval, the attack had been everywhere checked, and our troops — what was left of them — were back again in their old line. They had struck the core of the main German defence.

In this stubborn action against impossible odds the gallantry was so universal and absolute that it is idle to select special cases. In each mile there were men who performed the incredible. Nearly every English, Scots and Irish regiment was represented, as well as Midland and London Territorials, a gallant little company of Rhodesians, and a Newfoundland battalion drawn from the hard-bitten fishermen of that iron coast, who lost terribly on the slopes of Beaumont Hamel. Repeatedly the German position was pierced. At Serre fragments of two battalions pushed as far as Pendant Copse, 2,000 yards from the British lines.

North of Thiepval troops broke through the enemy trenches, passed the crest of the ridge and reached the point called The Crucifix, in rear of the first German position.

Not the least gallant of these exploits was that of the Ulster Division at the death-trap where the slopes south of Beaumont Hamel sink to the Ancre. It was the anniversary day of the Battle of the Boyne, and that charge when the men shouted "Remember the

Boyne" will be for ever a glorious page in the annals of Ireland. The Royal Irish Fusiliers were first out of the trenches. The Royal Irish Rifles followed them over the German parapets, bayoneting the machine-gunners, and the Inniskillings cleared the trenches to which they had given Irish names. Enfiladed on three sides they went on through successive German lines, and only a remnant came back to tell the tale. That remnant brought many prisoners, one man herding fifteen of the enemy through their own *barrage*.

In the words of the General who commanded it:

"The division carried out every portion of its allotted task in spite of the heaviest losses. It captured nearly 600 prisoners and carried its advance triumphantly to the limits of the objective laid down."

Nothing finer was done in the war. The splendid troops, drawn from those volunteers who had banded themselves together for another cause, now shed their blood like water for the liberty of the world.

That grim struggle from Thiepval northward was responsible for by far the greater number of the Allied losses of the day. But, though costly, it was not fruitless, for it occupied the bulk of the German defence. It was the price which had to be paid for the advance of the rest of the front. For, while in the north the living wave broke vainly and gained little, in the south "by creeks and inlets making" the tide was flowing strongly shoreward.

*

The map will show that Fricourt forms a bold salient; and it was the Allied purpose not to assault this salient but to cut it off. An advance on Ovillers and La Boisselle and up the long shallow depression towards Contalmaison, which our men called Sausage Valley, would, if united with the carrying of Mametz, pinch it so tightly that it must fall.

Ovillers and La Boisselle were strongly fortified villages, and on this first day, while we won the outskirts and carried the entrenchments before them, we did not control the ruins which our guns had pounded out of the shape of habitable dwellings. Just west of Fricourt a division was engaged which had suffered grave misfortunes at Loos. That day it got its own back, for it made no mistake, but poured resolutely into the angle east of Sausage Valley.

Before evening Mametz fell. Its church stood up, a broken tooth of masonry among the shattered houses, with an amphitheatre of splintered woods behind and around it. South of it ran a high road, and south of the road lay a little hill, with the German trench lines on the southern side. The division which took the place was one of the most famous in the British Army. It had fought at First Ypres, at Festubert and at Loos. Since the autumn of 1914 it had been changed in its composition, but there were in it battalions which had been for twenty months in the field. The whole division, old and new alike, went forward to their task as if it were their first day of war. On the slopes of the little hill three battalions advanced in line — one from a southern English county, one from a northern city, one of Highland regulars. They carried everything before them, and to one who followed their track the regularity of their advance was astonishing, for the dead lay aligned as if on some parade.

Montauban fell early in the day. The British lines lay in the hollow north of the Albert-Peronne road, where stands the hamlet of Carnoy. On the crest of the ridge beyond lay Montauban, now, like most Santerre villages, a few broken walls set among splintered trees. The brickfields on the right were expected to be the scene of a fierce struggle, but, to our amazement, they had been so shattered by our guns that they were taken easily. The Montauban attack was the most perfect of the episodes of the day. The artillery had done its work, and the 6th Bavarian Regiment opposed to us lost 3,000 out of a total strength of 3,500. The division which formed the British right wing advanced in parade order to a speedy success. Here is an extract from a soldier's narrative:

As we were going into Montauban we saw a German machine-gunner up a tree. He'd got the neatest little platform you ever saw, painted so that it was almost invisible. We shot him down, but he didn't fall clear, and the last we saw of him he was hanging by his boots from the branches…The spirit of our boys was splendid. They simply loved the show. One of them got blown up by a shell. He seemed pretty dazed, but he picked himself up and came along. All he said was, "Oh, there must be a war on after all, I suppose."

At that point was seen a sight hitherto unwitnessed in the campaign — the advance in line of the troops of Britain and France. On the British right lay a French Army, whose left wing was the famous "iron" Corps — the Corps which had held the Grand Couronne of Nancy in the feverish days of the Marne battle, and which by its counter-attack at Douaumont on that snowy 26th of February had turned the tide at Verdun.

It was the "Division de Fer" itself which moved in line with the British — horizon-blue beside khaki, and behind both the comforting bark of the incomparable "75's."

From the point of junction for eight miles southward the French advanced with lightning speed and complete success. The enemy was taken unawares. Officers were captured shaving in the dug-outs, whole battalions were rounded up, and all was done with the minimum of loss. One French regiment had two casualties; 800 was the total of one division. Long ere the evening the French were on the edge of Hardecourt and Curlu, and the villages of Dompierre, Becquincourt, Bussu and Fay were in their hands.

The German first position in its entirety had been captured from Mametz to Fay, a front of fourteen miles. Some 6,000 prisoners fell to the Allies, and great quantities of guns and stores. In the powdered trenches, in the woods and fields behind, and in the labyrinth of ruined dwellings the German dead lay thick. "That is the purpose of the battle," said a French soldier. "We do not want guns, for Krupp can make them faster than we can take them. But Krupp cannot make men."

To walk over the captured ground was to learn a

profound respect for the beaver-like industry of the German soldier. His fatigue-work must have reached the heroic scale. The old firing trenches were so badly smashed by our guns that it was hard to follow them, but what was left was good. The soil of the place is the best conceivable for digging, for it cuts like cheese, and hardens like brick in dry weather. The map shows a ramification of little red lines, but only the actual sight of that labyrinth could give a due impression of its strength. One communication trench, for example, was a tunnel a hundred yards long, lined with timber throughout, and so deep as to be beyond the reach of the heaviest shells. The small manholes used for snipers' posts were skilfully contrived.

Tunnels led to them from the trenches, and the openings were artfully screened by casual-looking debris. But the greatest marvels were the dug-outs. One at Fricourt had nine rooms and five bolt-holes; it had iron doors, gas curtains, linoleum on the floors, wallpaper and pictures on the walls, and boasted a good bathroom, electric light and electric bells.

The staff which occupied it must have lived in luxury. Many of these dug-outs had two-storeys, a thirty foot staircase, beautifully furnished, leading to the first suite, and a second stair of the same length conducting to a lower storey. In such places machine-guns could be protected during any bombardment. But the elaboration of such dwellings went far beyond military needs. When the Germans boasted that their front on the West was impregnable they sincerely believed it. They thought they had established a continuing city, from which they would emerge only at a triumphant peace. The crumbling — not of their front trenches only but of their whole first position — was such a shock as King Priam's court must have received when the Wooden Horse disgorged the Greeks in the heart of their citadel.

It was not won without stark fighting. The Allied soldiers were quick to kindle in the fight, and more formidable figures than those bronzed steel-hatted warriors history has never seen on a field of battle. Those who witnessed the charge of the Highlanders at Loos were not likely to forget its fierce resolution. Said a French officer who was present: "I don't know what effect it had on the Boche, but it made *my* blood run cold." Our men were fighting against the foes of humanity and they did not make war as a joke. But there was none of the savagery which comes either from a half-witted militarism or from rattled nerves. The Germans had been officially told that the English took no prisoners, and this falsehood, while it made the stouter fellows fight to the death, sent scores of poor creatures huddling in dug-outs, from which they had to be extracted like shell-fish. But, after surrender, there was no brutality — very much the reverse. As one watched the long line of wounded — the "walking cases" — straggling back from the firing line to a dressing-station, they might have been all of one side. One picture remains in the memory. Two wounded Gordon Highlanders were hobbling along, and supported between them a wounded Badener. The last seen of the trio was that the Scots were giving him water and cigarettes, and he was cutting buttons from his tunic as souvenirs for his comforters. A letter of an officer on this point is worth quoting:

"The more I see of war the more I am convinced of the fundamental decency of our own folk. They may have a crude taste in music and art and things of that sort; they may lack the patient industry of the Boche; but for sheer goodness of heart, for kindness to all unfortunate things, like prisoners, wounded, animals and ugly women, they fairly beat the band."

It is the kind of tribute which most Britons would prefer to any other.

Sunday, the 2nd of July, was a day of level heat, in which the dust stood in steady walls on every road behind the front and in the tortured areas of the captured ground. The success of the Saturday had, as we have seen, put our right well in advance of our centre, and it was necessary to bring forward the left part of the line from Thiepval to Fricourt so as to make the breach in the German position uniform over a broad enough front. Accordingly, all that day there was a fierce struggle at Ovillers and La Boisselle. At the former village we won the entrenchments before it, and late in the evening we succeeded in entering the labyrinth of cellars, the ruins of what had been La Boisselle. As yet there was no counterattack. The surprise in the south had been too great, and the Germans had not yet brought up their reserve divisions. All that day squadrons of Allied airplanes bombed depots and lines of communications in the German hinterland. The long echelons of the Allied "sausages" glittered in the sun, but only one German kite balloon could be detected. We had found a way of bombing those fragile gas-bags and turning them into wisps of flame. The Fokkers strove in vain to check our airmen, and at least two were brought crashing to the earth.

At 2 in the afternoon of Sunday Fricourt fell, the taking of Mametz and the positions won in the Fricourt Wood to the east had made its capture certain. During the night part of the garrison slipped out, but when our men entered it, bombing from house to house, they made a great haul of prisoners and guns. "Like a Belfast riot on the top of Vesuvius," was an Irish soldier's description of the fight. Further south the French continued their victorious progress. They destroyed a German counterattack on the new position at Hardecourt; they took Curlu; and, south of the river, they took Frise and the wood of Méreaucourt beyond it. They did more, for at many points between the river and Assevilliers they broke into the German second position.

On Monday, July 3rd, General von Below issued an order to his troops, which showed that, whatever the German Press might say, the German soldiers had no delusion as to the gravity of the Allied offensive.

"The decisive issue of the war depends on the victory of the 2nd Army on the Somme. We must win this battle in spite of the enemy's temporary superiority in artillery and infantry. The important ground lost in certain places will be recaptured by our attack after the arrival of reinforcements. The vital thing

is to hold on to our present positions at all costs and to improve them. I forbid the voluntary evacuation of trenches. The will to stand firm must be impressed on every man in the army. The enemy should have to carve his way over heaps of corpses...I require commanding officers to devote their utmost energies to the establishment of order behind the front."

Von Below had correctly estimated the position. The old ground, with all it held, must be re-won if possible; no more must be lost; fresh lines must be constructed in the rear. But the new improvised lines could be no equivalent of those mighty fastnesses which represented the work of eighteen months. Therefore those fastnesses must be regained. We shall learn how ill his enterprise prospered.

For a correct understanding of the position on Monday, July 3rd, it is necessary to recall the exact alignment of the new British front. It fell into two sections. The first lay from Thiepval to Fricourt, and was bisected by the Albert-Bapaume road, which ran like an arrow over the watershed. Here Thiepval, Ovillers, and La Boisselle were positions in the German first line. Contalmaison, to the east of La Boisselle, was a strongly fortified village on high ground, which formed, so to speak, a pivot in the

German intermediate line — the line which covered their field-guns. The second position ran through Pozières to the two Bazentins. On the morning of July 3rd the British had not got Thiepval, nor Ovillers; they had only a portion of La Boisselle, but south of it they had broken through the first position and were well on the road to Contalmaison. All this northern section consisted of bare undulating slopes — once covered with crops, but now like some lunar desert where life was forbidden. Everywhere it was seamed with the scars of trenches and pock-marked with shell holes. The few trees lining the roads had been long razed, and the only vegetation was coarse grass, thistles, and the ubiquitous poppy and mustard.

The southern section, from Fricourt to Montauban, was of a different character. It was patched with large woods, curiously clean cut like the copses in the park of a country-house. A line of them ran from Fricourt northeastward — Fricourt Wood, Bottom Wood, the big wood of Mametz, the woods of Bazentin, and the wood of Foureaux, which our men called High Wood; while from Montauban ran a second line, the woods of Bernafay and Trônes and Delville Wood around Longueval. Here all the German first position had been captured. The second position ran through the Bazentins, Longueval, and Guillemont, but to reach it some difficult woodland country had to be traversed. On July 3rd, therefore, the southern half of the British line was advancing against the enemy's second position, while the northern half had still for its objective Ovillers and La Boisselle in the first position and the intermediate point, Contalmaison.

*

It will be most convenient to take the two sections separately, since their problems were different, and see the progress of the British advance in each, preparatory to the assault on the enemy's second position. In the north our task was to capture the three fortified places, Ovillers, La Boisselle and Contalmaison, which were on a large scale the equivalent of the *fortins*, manned by machine-guns, which we had known to our cost at Festubert and Loos. Thiepval on the extreme left was less important, for the high ground could be won without its capture. The German troops in this area obeyed to the full von Below's instructions and fought hard for every inch. On the night of Sunday, July 2nd, La Boisselle was penetrated, and all Monday the struggle swayed around that village and Ovillers. La

Boisselle lies on the light of the high road; Ovillers is to the north and a little to the east, separated by a dry hollow which we called Mash Valley. All Monday night the struggle see-sawed, our troops winning ground and the Germans winning back small portions. On Tuesday, the 4th, the heat wave broke in thunderstorms and torrential rain, and the dusty hollows became quagmires. That evening La Boisselle was won, after one of the bloodiest contests of the war.

On Wednesday and Thursday, the old enemy first line, which we held just south of Thiepval, was the subject of a heavy bombardment and various counter-attacks. On Friday, July 7th, came the first big advance on Contalmaison from Sausage Valley on the southwest, and from the tangle of copses northeast of Fricourt, through which ran the Fricourt-Contalmaison high road. On the latter side good work had already been done, the enemy *fortins* at Birch Tree Wood and Shelter Copse having been taken on July 5th, and the work called the Quadrangle on July 6th. On the Friday the attack ranged from the Leipzig Redoubt, south of Thiepval, and the environs of Ovillers to the skirts of Contalmaison. About noon our infantry, after a heavy initial bombardment, carried Contalmaison by storm, releasing a small party of Tyneside Scottish, who had been made prisoners four days earlier. The 3rd Prussian Guard Division were our opponents — containing true Guards regiments, not like the 2nd Guards Reserve Division, which had been against us at Serre on July 1st, which was only a division used as a reserve to the Guards. They were heavily punished, and 700 of them fell as prisoners into our hands. But our success at Contalmaison was beyond our strength to maintain, and in the afternoon a counter-attack forced us out of the village. That same day we had pushed our front nearly half-a-mile along the Bapaume road, east of La Boisselle, and had taken most of the Leipzig Redoubt. Ovillers was now in danger of envelopment. One brigade had attacked in front, and another brigade, pressing in on the flank, was cutting the position in two. All that day there was a deluge of rain, and the sodden ground and flooded trenches crippled the movement of our men.

Next day the struggle for Ovillers continued. The place was now a mass of battered trenches, rubble, and muddy shell-holes, and every yard had to be fought for. We were also slowly consolidating our ground around Contalmaison, and driving the Germans from their strongholds in the little copses. Ever since July 7th we had held the southern corner of the village. On the night of Monday, the 10th, pushing from Bailiff's Wood on the west side in four successive waves, with our guns lifting the range in front of us, we broke into the northwest corner, swept round on the north, and after bitter hand-to-hand fighting conquered the whole village. As for Ovillers, it was now surrounded and beyond succour, and it was only a question of days till its stubborn garrison must yield. It did not actually fall till Monday, July 17th, when the gallant remnant — two officers and 124 guardsmen — surrendered. By that time our main push had swept far to the eastward.

A good description of the country over which we had advanced is contained in a letter of an officer to a friend who had been invalided home:

"I suppose it would seem nothing to other people, but you, who were here with us through all those dismal winter months, will understand how thrilling it was to be able to walk about on that ground in broad daylight, smoking one's pipe. You remember how our chaps used to risk their lives in the early days for such silly souvenirs as nose-caps and that kind of thing. You could gather them by the cartload now, and Boche caps and buttons, and bits of uniform and boots, and broken rifles and odd tags of equipment — cartloads of it. To other folk, and on the maps, one place seems just like another, I suppose; but to us

— La Boiselle and Ovillers — my hat! To walk about in those hells! Not one of those broken walls we knew so well (through our glasses) is standing now; and only a few jagged spikes where the trees were. I went along the 'sunken road' all the way to Contalmaison. Talk about sacred ground. When I think what that no-man's-land was to us for nearly a year! The new troops coming up now go barging across it in the most light-hearted way. They know nothing about it. It means no more to them than the roads behind used to mean to us. It's all behind, to them, and never was the front. But when I think how we watered every yard of it with blood and sweat! Children might play there now, if it didn't look so much like the aftermath of an earthquake. But you know there's a kind of a wrench about seeing the new chaps swagger over it so carelessly, and seeing it gradually merged into the 'behind the line' country. I have a sort of feeling it ought to be marked off somehow, a permanent memorial.

"You remember that old couple who had the blacksmith's shop at —. The wife was down at the corner by — the other night, when I came along with half the platoon. I found her wringing the hands of some of our stolid chaps, and couldn't make it out. Then she told me, half sobbing, how she and her husband owned a couple of fields just beyond our old front line, and how she wanted to thank us for getting them back. Think what those fields must have been in the spring of 1914, and what *they are to-day, every yard of them torn by shells, burrowed through and through by old trenches and dug-outs; think of the hundreds of tons of wire, sand-bags, timber, galvanized iron, duck-boards, revetting stuff, steel, iron, blood and sweat, the rum jars, bully beef tins, old trench boots, field dressings, cartridge cases, rockets, wire stanchions and stakes, gas gongs, bomb boxes, S.A.A. cases, broken canteens, bits of uniforms, and buried soldiers, and Boches — all in the old lady's two little fields. Think how she must have felt, after two years, to know we'd got them back. She's walked over them by now, I daresay."*

*

To turn to the southern sector, where the problem was to clear out the fortified woods which intervened between us and the German second line. From the crest of the first ridge above Fricourt and Montauban one looks into a shallow trough, called Caterpillar Valley, beyond which the ground rises to the Bazentin-Longueval ridge. On the left, toward Contalmaison, is the big Mametz Wood; to the right, beyond Montauban, the pear-shaped woods of Bernafay and Trônes.

On Monday, the 3rd, the ground east of Fricourt Wood was cleared, and the approaches to Mametz Wood won. That day a German counter-attack developed. A fresh division appeared at Montauban, which was faithfully handled by our guns. The "milking of the line" had begun, for a battalion from the Champagne front appeared east of Mametz early on Monday morning. Within a very short time of detraining at railhead the whole battalion had been destroyed or made prisoners. In one small area over 1,000 men were taken. A wounded officer of a Highland regiment has described the scene:

"It was the finest show I ever saw in my life. There were six hundred Boches of all ranks marching in column of route across the open back towards our rear. They were disarmed, of course. And what do you think they had for escort? Three ragged Jocks of our battalion, all blood and dirt and rags, with their rifles at the slope, doing a sort of G.O.C.'s inspection parade march, like pipers at the head of a battalion. That was good enough for me. I brought up the rear, and that's how I got to a dressing-station and had my arm dressed. I walked behind a six hundred strong column of Boches, but I couldn't equal the swagger of those three Jocks in the lead."

Next day, Tuesday, July 4th, we were well established in the Wood of Mametz, 3,000 yards north of Mametz village, and by midday had taken the Wood of Bernafay.

These intermediate positions were not acquired without a grim struggle. The woods were thick with undergrowth which had not been cut for two seasons, and though our artillery played havoc with the trees it could not clear away the tangled shrubbery beneath them. The Germans had filled the place with machine-gun redoubts, connected by concealed trenches, and in some cases they had machine-guns in positions in the trees. Each step in our advance had to be fought for, and in that briery labyrinth the battle tended always to become a series of individual combats. Every position we won was subjected at once to a heavy counter-bombardment. During the first two days of July it was possible to move in moderate safety almost up to the British firing-lines, but from the 4th onward the enemy kept up a steady bombardment of our whole new front, and *barraged* heavily in all the hinterland around Fricourt, Mametz and Montauban.

On Saturday, July 8th, we made our first lodgement in the Wood of Trônes, assisted by the flanking fire of the French guns. We took 130 prisoners, and broke up the German counterattacks. For the next five days that wood was the hottest corner in the southern British sector. Slowly and stubbornly we pushed our way northwards from our point of lodgement in the southern end. Six counter-attacks were launched against us on Sunday night and Monday, and on Monday afternoon the sixth succeeded in winning back some of the wood. These desperate efforts exactly suited our purpose, for the German losses under our artillery fire were enormous. The fighting was continued on Tuesday, when we recaptured the whole of the wood except the extreme northern corner. That same day we approached the north end of Mametz Wood and took a "dump" of German stores. The difficulty of the fighting and the strength of the defence may be realised from the fact that the taking of a few hundred yards or so of woodland meant invariably the capture of several hundred prisoners.

By Wednesday evening, July 12th, we had taken the whole of Mametz Wood. Its 200 odd acres, interlaced with barbed wire, honeycombed with trenches, and bristling with machine-guns, had given us a tough struggle, especially the last strip on the north side, where the German *minenwerfers* were thick, and their machine-gun positions enfiladed every advance. At 4 o'clock in the afternoon we broke out of the wood, and were face to face at last with the main German second position. Meantime, the Wood of Trônes had become a Tom Tiddler's Ground, which neither antagonist could fully claim or use as a base. It was at the mercy of the artillery fire of both sides, and it was impossible in the time to construct shell-proof defences.

In the French section the advance had been swift and continuous. At the beginning of the battle they had been faced with 27 German battalions, principally of the 17th Corps. The attack, as we have seen, was a complete surprise, for half-an-hour before it began on July 1st, an order was issued to the German troops, predicting the imminent fall of Verdun, and announcing that a French offensive elsewhere had thereby been prevented. On the nine-mile front from Maricourt to Estrées the German first position had been carried the first day. The heavy guns, when they had sufficiently pounded it, ceased their fire; then the "75's" took up the tale and plastered the front and communication trenches with shrapnel; then a skirmishing line advanced to report the damage done; and finally the infantry moved forward to an easy occupation. It had been the German method at Verdun; but it was practised by the French with far greater precision, and with far better fighting material. On Monday, July 3rd, they were into the German second position south of the Somme. By the next day they had taken Belloy-en-Santerre, a point in the third line. On Wednesday they had the better part of Estrées and were within three miles of Peronne. Counterattacks by the 17th Bavarian Division achieved nothing, and the German rail-head was moved from Peronne to Chaulnes. On the night of Sunday, July 9th, they took Biaches, a mile from Peronne, and held a front from there to Barleux — a position beyond the German third line. There was now nothing in front of them in this section except the line of the Upper Somme. This was south of the river. North of it they had attained points in the second line, but had not yet carried it wholly from Hem northwards.

The next step was for the British to attack the enemy second position before them. It ran, as we have seen, from Pozières through the Bazentins and Longueval to Guillemont. On Thursday, July 13th, we were in a condition to begin the next stage of our advance. The capture of Contalmaison had been the indispensable preliminary, and immediately following its fall Sir Douglas Haig issued his first summary. "After ten days and nights of continuous fighting, our troops have completed the methodical capture of the whole of the enemy's first system of defence on a front of 14,000 yards. This system of defence consisted of numerous and continuous lines of fire trenches, extending to various depths of from 2,000 to 4,000 yards, and included five strongly fortified villages, numerous heavily wired and entrenched woods, and a large number of immensely strong redoubts. The capture of each of these trenches represented an operation of some importance, and the whole of them are now in our hands." The summary did not err from overstatement. If the northern part of our front, from Thiepval to Gommecourt, had not succeeded, the southern part had steadily bitten its way like a deadly acid into as strong a position as any *terrain* of the campaign could show. We had already attracted against us the bulk of the available German reserves, and had largely destroyed them. The strength of our plan lay in its deliberateness, and the mathematical sequence of its stages.

CHAPTER THREE – THE SECOND STAGE

At dawn on Friday, the 14th, began the second stage of the battle.

The most methodical action has its gambling element, its moments when a risk must be boldly taken. Without such hazards there can be no chance of surprise. The British attack of July 14th had much of this calculated audacity. In certain parts — as at Contalmaison Villa and Mametz Wood — we held positions within a few hundred yards of the enemy's line. But in the section from Bazentin-le-Grand to Longueval there was a long advance before us up the slopes north of Caterpillar Valley. On the extreme right the Wood of Trônes gave us a somewhat indifferent place of assembly.

The difficulties before the British attack were so great that more than one distinguished French officer doubted its possibility. One British General, in conversation with a French colleague, undertook, if the thing did not succeed, to eat his hat. When about noon on the 14th the French General heard what had happened, he is reported to have observed: "C'est bien! Le General X ne mange pas son chapeau!" It was a pleasant reflection for the British troops that they had surprised their Allies; France had so often during the campaign exceeded the wildest expectations of her friends.

The day of the attack was of fortunate omen, for the 14th of July was the anniversary of the fall of the Bastille, the fete-day of France. In Paris there was such a parade as that city had not seen in its long history — a procession of Allied troops, Belgians, Russians, British infantry, and last of all, the blue-coated heroes of France's incomparable line. It was a shining proof to the world of the unity of the Alliance. And on the same day, while the Paris crowd was cheering the Scottish pipers as they swung down the boulevards, the British troops in Picardy were breaking through the German line, crying *Vive la France!* in all varieties of accent. It was France's Day in the eyes of every soldier, the sacred day of that people whom in farm and village and trench they had come to reverence and love.

The front chosen for attack was from a point southeast of Pozières to Longueval and Delville Wood, a space of some four miles. Incidentally, it was necessary for our right flank to clear out the Wood of Trônes. Each village in the second line had its adjacent or enfolding wood — Bazentin-le-Petit, Bazentin-le-Grand, and at Longueval the big wood of Delville. In the centre, a mile and more beyond the German position, the wood of Foureaux, which we called High Wood, hung like a dark cloud on the sky line.

It was only the day before that we had consolidated our new line, and the work required to prepare for the attack was colossal. The Germans did not believe in an immediate assault, and when the bombardment began they thought it was no more than one of the spasmodic "preparations" with which we had already cloaked our purpose. In the small hours of the morning our guns opened and continued in a crescendo till 3.20 a.m., when the final hurricane fell. An observer has described the spectacle:

"It was a thick night, the sky veiled in clouds, mottled and hurrying clouds, through which only one planet shone serene and steadily high up in the eastern sky. But the wonderful and appalling thing was the belt of flame which fringed a great arc of the horizon before us. It was not, of course, a steady flame, but it was one which never went out, rising and falling, flashing and flickering, half dimmed with its own smoke, against which the

stabs and jets of fire from the bursting shells flared out intensely white or dully orange. Out of it all, now here, now there, rose like fountains the great balls of star shells and signal lights — theirs or ours — white and crimson and green, The noise of the shells was terrific, and when the guns near us spoke, not only the air but the earth beneath us shook. All the while, too, overhead, amid all the clamour and shock, in the darkness and no less as night paled to day, the larks sang. Only now and again would the song be audible, but whenever there was an interval between the roaring of the nearer guns, above all the distant tumult, it came down clear and very beautiful by contrast, Nor was the lark the only bird that was awake, for close by us, somewhere in the dark, a quail kept constantly urging us — or the guns — to be Quick-be-quick. "

*

Just before 8.30 a.m., when the cloudy dawn had fully come, the infantry attacked. In some places they had had to cover a long distance before reaching their striking-point. So complete was the surprise that, in the dark the battalions which had the furthest road to go came within 200 yards of the enemy's wire with scarcely a casualty. When the German *barrage* came it fell behind them. There were three sections of the main attack — the division which had taken Mametz, against Bazentin-le-Petit; a famous regular division, which had fought in the Peninsula, against Bazentin-le-Grand; and a Scottish new division, against Longueval village and Delville Wood. In the last division was a brigade of South African troops who had been in the Damaraland Campaign.

The attack failed nowhere. In some parts it was slower than others — where the enemy's defence had been less comprehensively destroyed, but by the afternoon all our tasks had been accomplished. To take one instance. Two of the attacking brigades were each composed of two battalions of the New Army and two of the old Regulars. The general commanding put the four new battalions into the first line. The experiment proved the worth of the new troops, for a little after midday their work was done, their part of the German second line was taken, and 662 unwounded men, 36 officers (including a battalion commander), 4 howitzers, 4 field-guns, and 14 machine-guns were in their hands. By the evening we had the whole second line from Bazentin-le-Petit to Longueval, and in the twenty-four hours' battle we took over 2,000 prisoners, many of them of the 3rd Division of the German Guards. The audacious enterprise had been crowned with an unparalleled success.

The Wood of Trônes on our right flank was cleared, and in that place occurred one of the most romantic incidents of the action. On Thursday night an attack had been delivered there, and 100 men of the Royal West Kents became separated from their battalion. They had machine-guns with them and sufficient ammunition, so they were able to fortify one or two posts which they maintained all night against tremendous odds. Next morning the British sweep retrieved them, and the position they had maintained gave our troops invaluable aid in the clearing of the wood. All through this Battle of the Somme there were similar incidents; an advance would go too far and the point would be cut off, but that point would succeed in maintaining itself till a fresh advance reclaimed it. A better proof of discipline and resolution could not be desired.

On Saturday, July 15th, we were busy consolidating the ground won, and at some points pushing further. Our aircraft, in spite of the haze, were never idle, and in twenty-four hours they destroyed four Fokkers, three biplanes, and a double-engined plane, without the loss of a single machine. On the left we fought our way to the skirts of Pozières. We took the whole of Bazentin-le-Petit Wood and beat off two counter-attacks. In the centre, north of Bazentin-le-Grand, we pushed as far as High Wood, and broke into the German third line. It was late in the afternoon when the advance was made, the first in eighteen months which had seen the use of cavalry. In the Champagne battle of September 25th the French had used some squadrons of General Baratier's Colonial Horse in the ground between the first and second German lines to sweep up prisoners and capture guns. This tactical expedient was now followed by the British, with the difference that in Champagne the fortified second line had not been taken, while in Picardy we were through all the main fortifications and operating against an improvised position. The cavalry used were a troop of the Dragoon Guards and a troop of Deccan Horse. They made their way up the shallow valley beyond Bazentin-le-Grand, finding cover in the slope of the ground and the growing corn. The final advance was made partly on foot and partly on horseback, and the enemy in the corn were ridden down, captured, or slain with lance and sabre. The cavalry then set to work to entrench themselves, to protect the flank of the advancing infantry in High Wood. It was a clean and workmanlike job, and the news of it exhilarated the whole line. That cavalry should be used at all seemed to forecast the end of the long trench fighting and the beginning of a campaign in the open.

On the right, around Longueval and in Delville Wood, there was the fiercest struggle of all. By the Saturday evening the whole wood had been taken, but the enemy was still in possession of certain orchards on the high ground to the north of the village, on the road to Flers. The position was well suited for counter-attacks, and was much at the mercy of the enemy's guns. For four days the South African Brigade and the Scots wrestled in the wood, desperate hand-to-hand fighting such as the American armies knew in the last Wilderness campaign. Their assault had been splendid, but their defence was a far greater exploit. They hung on with little food and water, exposed to an incessant bombardment, and, when their ranks were terribly depleted, they flung back an attack by three Brandenburg regiments. In this far-flung battle all parts of the Empire won fame, and not least was the glory of the South African contingent.

In this stage of the action we tried conclusions with two of the most celebrated of the German formations. For some days we had engaged the 3rd Guards Division — that division which in April had been brought from the Russian front, and had been hailed by the Kaiser as the hope of his throne and empire. It contained three regiments — the Guards Fusiliers, the Lehr Regiment, and the 9th Grenadiers — and every one had been heavily depleted. Some of them showed fine fighting quality, such as the garrison at Ovillers, but they met something more than their match in our New Army. In the attack on the second position the 5th Brandenburg Division appeared, that division which had attacked at Douaumont on February 25th and at Vaux on March 9th. Now it was virtually a new formation, for at Verdun it had lost well over 100 per cent, of its original strength. It was scarcely more fortunate at Longueval. "The enemy," said the Kaiser, in his address on April 20th, "has prepared his own soup, and now he must sup it, and I look to you to see to it. May the appearance of the 3rd Guards Division inform him what soldiers are facing him." The information had been conveyed to us, and our men were by no means depressed. They desired to meet with the best that Germany could produce, for they were confident that they could put that best out of action.

On Sunday, the 16th, we withdrew our advanced posts from High Wood. They had done their work, and formed a screen behind which we had consolidated our line. On Monday Ovillers was at last completely taken after a stout defence, and the way was prepared for a general assault on Pozières. That day, too, on our right we widened the gap in the German front by the capture of Waterlot Farm, half-way between Longueval and Guillemont. The weather had again broken, and drenching rain and low mists made progress difficult. The enemy had got up many new batteries, whose position could not be detected in such weather by our aircraft. He himself was better off, since we were fighting on ground he had once held, and he had the register of our trench lines and most of our possible gun positions.

The total of unwounded prisoners in British hands was now 189 officers and 10,779 men. The armament taken included five 8 in. and three 6 in. howitzers, four 6 in. guns, five other heavies, 37 field guns, 30 trench mortars and 66 machine-guns. Of the German losses in dead and wounded no exact estimate is possible, but they were beyond doubt very great, and their abortive counter-attacks had probably brought up the total of the defence to a figure as high as that of the attack.

Captured letters all told the same tale. Instant relief was begged for; one battalion consisted of three officers, two N.C.O.'s, and nineteen men; another was so exhausted that it could no longer be employed in fighting; another had completely lost its fighting spirit.

No British soldier decried the quality of his opponents. At the most he declared that it was "patchy," which was the truth. "The way some of 'em talk," said a young officer, "you might think the Boches were all baby-killers, frightened of their own shadows, and anxious only to be taken prisoners.

Well, of course, I know there are some like that, a good many in fact, and in all. the British Army I don't believe there's one. Anyhow, I've never seen or heard of a British soldier running out with hands up, calling for mercy and giving himself up. Never heard of it, and I saw Boches doing it, saw a Boche officer doing it. But mind you, the fellows we ran up against fought like tigers. I say they were good soldiers, and brave men.

We were between Fricourt and Mametz, and when we had the Boche with his back to the wall he fought like a tiger-cat. No *Kamarade* business about that. They were shying bombs in our faces at point-blank range when our bayonets were absolutely touching 'em."

There were extraordinarily gallant elements in the German ranks, but they were watered down with much indifferent stuff. Many had lost heart for the fight; they had been told so often of victory assured that they ended by disbelieving everything.

On one occasion a hundred men put up their hands while actually charging. Distressful letters from their homes, a lack of confidence in their officers and enthusiasm for their cause, and the suspicion which comes from a foolish censoring of all truth, had impaired the fibre of men who in normal circumstances would have fought stoutly. The German machine was still formidable, but its motive power was weakening.

As for the Allies every day that passed nerved and steeled them. The French had made the final resolution and the ultimate sacrifice. There was no alternative but victory, and the whole race was ready to perish on the battlefield sooner than accept a German domination. Of the same quality was the British temper.

"Most of these men," said a chaplain, "never handled a gun till they joined up. Yet they have faced bigger things than any veteran ever faced before, and faced them steadily, seeing it all very clearly and fearing it not one scrap; though they have again and again forced mad fear into the highly trained troops facing them.

That is because they have something that you cannot make in foundries, that you cannot even give by training. I could give it a name the Church would recognise. Let's say they know their cause is good, as they very surely do. The Germans may write on their badges that God is with them, but our lads — they know."

The next step was to round off our capture of the enemy second position, and consolidate our ground, for it was very certain that the Germans would not be content to leave us in quiet possession. The second line being lost from east of Pozières to Delville Wood, the enemy was compelled to make a switch line to connect his third position with an uncaptured point in his second, such as Pozières. Fighting continued in the skirts of Delville Wood, and among the orchards of Longueval, which had to be taken one by one. Apart from this general activity, our two main objectives were Pozières and Guillemont. The first, with the Windmill beyond it, represented the highest ground of the Thiepval plateau; the second was necessary to us before we could align our next advance with that of the French. Our aim was the crest of the ridge, the watershed, which would give us direct observation over all the rolling country to the east. The vital points on this watershed were Mouquet Farm, between Thiepval and Pozières; the Windmill, now only a stone pedestal, on the high road east of Pozières; High Wood, and the high ground direct east of Longueval.

The weather did not favour us. The third week of July was rain and fog. The last week and the first fortnight of August saw blazing summer weather, which in that arid and dusty land told severely on men wearing heavy steel helmets and carrying a load of equipment. There was little wind, and a heat-haze lay low on the uplands. This meant poor visibility at a time when air reconnaissance was most vital. Hence the task of counter-bombardment grew very difficult, and the steps in our progress became for the moment slow and irregular. A battle which advances without a hitch exists only in a Staff college *kriegspiel* and the wise general, in preparing his plans, makes ample allowance for delays. On July 19th there was an attempt on Guillemont from Trônes Wood which failed to progress. On the 20th the French made fine progress, pushing their front east of Hardecourt beyond the Combles-Clèry light railway, and south of the Somme widening the gap by carrying the whole German defence system from Barleux to Vermandovillers. For the next two days our guns bombarded the whole enemy front, and on the Sunday, July 23rd, came the next great infantry attack.

That attack had a wide front, but its main fury was on the left, where Pozières and its Windmill crowned the slope up which ran the Albert-Bapaume road. The village had long ere this been pounded flat, the Windmill was a stump, and the trees in the gardens matchwood, but every yard of those devastated acres was fortified in the German fashion with covered trenches, deep dug-outs and machine-gun emplacements.

The assault was delivered from two sides — the Midland Territorials moving from the southwest in the ground between Pozières and Ovillers, and an Australian division from the southeast, advancing from the direction of Contalmaison Villa. The movement began about midnight, and the Midlanders speedily cleared out the defences which the Germans had flung out south of the village to the left of the highroad, and held a line along the outskirts of the place in the direction of Thiepval. The Australians had a difficult task — for they had first to take a sunken road parallel with the highway, then a formidable line of trenches, and finally the high road itself which runs straight through the middle of the village.

The Australian Corps was second to none in the new British Army. In the famous landing at Gallipoli and in a dozen desperate fights, culminating in the great battle which began on August 6th, 1915, they had shown themselves incomparable in the fire of assault and in reckless personal valour. In the grim struggle now beginning they had to face a far heavier fire and far more formidable defences than anything that Gallipoli could show. For their task not gallantry only but perfect discipline and perfect coolness were needed. The splendid troops were equal to the call. They won the high road after desperate fighting in the ruined houses, and established a line where the breadth of the road alone separated them from the enemy. A famous division of British regulars on their flank sent them a message to say that they were proud to fight by their side.

When all were gallant it is hard to select special incidents, but in their record of personal bravery the Australians in the West rivalled their famous attack on the Lone Pine position in Gallipoli. The list of Victoria Crosses awarded is sufficient proof. Second-Lieutenant Blackburn led four parties of bombers against a German stronghold and took 250 yards of trench. He then crawled forward with a sergeant to reconnoitre, and, returning, led his men to a capture of a further 120 yards. Private Thomas Cooke, a machine-gunner, went on firing when he was the only man left and was found dead beside his gun. Private William Jackson brought in wounded men from no-man's-land till his arm was blown off by a shell, and then, after obtaining assistance, went out again to find two wounded comrades. Private Martin O'Meara for four days brought in wounded under heavy fire, and carried ammunition to a vital point through an incessant *barrage*. Private John Leak was one of a party which captured a German stronghold. At one moment, when the enemy's bombs were outranging ours, he leaped from the trench, ran forward under close-range machine-gun fire, and bombed the enemy's post. He then jumped into the post and bayonetted three German bombers. Later, when the party was driven back by overwhelming numbers, he was at every stage the last to withdraw. "His courage was amazing," says the official report, "and had such an effect on the enemy that, on the arrival of reinforcements, the whole trench was recaptured."

On Monday and Tuesday the battle continued, and by the evening of the latter day most of Pozières was in our hands. By Wednesday morning, July 26th, the whole village was ours, and the Territorials on the left were pushing northward and had taken two lines of trenches. The two divisions joined hands at the north corner, where they occupied the cemetery, and held a portion of the switch line. Here they lived under a perpetual enemy bombardment. The Germans still held the Windmill, which was the higher ground and gave them a good observation point. The sight of that ridge from the road east of Ovillers was one that no man who saw it was likely to forget. It seemed to be smothered monotonously in smoke and fire. Wafts of the thick heliotrope smell of the lachrymatory shells floated down from it. Out of the dust and glare would come Australian units which had been relieved, long lean men with the shadows of a great fatigue around their deep-set far-sighted eyes. They were perfectly cheerful and composed, and no Lowland Scot was ever less inclined to expansive speech. At the most they would admit in their slow quiet voices that what they had been through had been "some battle."

An observer with the Australians has described the unceasing bombardment:

"Hour after hour, day and night, with increasing intensity as the time went on, the enemy rained heavy shell into the area. Now he would send them crashing in on a line south of the road — eight heavy shells at a time, minute after minute, followed by a burst of shrapnel. Now he would place a curtain straight

across this valley or that till the sky and landscape were blotted out, except for fleeting glimpses seen as through a lift of fog... Day and night the men worked through it, fighting the horrid machinery far over the horizon as if they were fighting Germans hand to hand; building up whatever it battered down; buried some of them, not once, but again and again and again. What is a barrage against such troops? They went through it as you would go through a summer shower, too proud to bend their heads, many of them, because their mates were looking. I am telling you of things I have seen. As one of the best of their officers said to me: 'I have to walk about as if I liked it; what else can you do when your own men teach you to?'"

Meantime there had been heavy fighting around Longueval and in Delville Wood. On Thursday, the 27th, the wood was finally cleared of the enemy, and next day the last enemy outpost, in Longueval village was captured. In this action we accounted for the remains of the Brandenburgers, taking prisoner three officers and one hundred and fifty-eight men. The British had not met them since that day on the Aisne, when they had been forced back by our 1st Division behind the edge of the plateau.

Early on the morning of Saturday, the 29th, the Australians attacked at Pozières towards the

Windmill, and after a fierce hand-to-hand struggle in the darkness advanced their front to the edge of the trench labyrinth which constituted that position. Next morning, we attacked Guillemont from the northwest and west, while the French pushed almost to the edge of Maurepas. Our farthest limit was the station on the light railway just outside Guillemont village.

Little happened for some days. The heat was now very great, so great that even men inured to an Australian summer found it hard to bear, and the maddening haze still muffled the landscape. The French were meantime fighting their way through the remnants of the German second position north of the Somme between Hem Wood and Monacu Farm. There were strong counter-attacks against Delville Wood, which were beaten off by our guns before they got to close range. Daily we bombarded points in the enemy hinterland and did much destruction among their dep6ts and billets and heavy batteries. And then on the night of Friday, August 4th, came the final attack at Pozières.

We had already won the German second position up to the top of the village, where the new switch line joined on. The attack was in the nature of a surprise. It began at nine in the evening, when the light was still strong. The Australians attacked on the right at the Windmill, and troops from South England on the left. The trenches, which had been almost obliterated by our guns, were carried at a rush, and before the darkness came we had taken the rest of the second position on a front of 2,000 yards. Counter-attacks followed all through the night, but they were badly co-ordinated and achieved nothing. On Saturday we had pushed our line north and west of the village from 400 to GOO yards on a front of 3,000. Early on Sunday morning the Germans counter-attacked with liquid lire and gained a small portion of the trench line, which was speedily recovered. The position was now that we held the much contested Windmill, and that we extended on the east of the village to the west end of the Switch, while west of Pozières we had pushed so far north that the German line was drooping like the eaves of a steep roof. We had taken some 600 prisoners, and at last we were looking over the watershed.

The following week saw repeated attempts by the enemy to recover his losses. The German bombardment was incessant and intense, and on the high bare scarp around the Windmill our troops had to make heavy drafts on their fortitude. On Tuesday, August 8th, the British right closed farther in on Guillemont. At Pozières, too, every day our lines advanced, especially in the angle toward Mouquet Farm, between the village and Thiepval. We were exposed to a flanking fire from Thiepval, and to the exactly ranged heavy batteries around Courcelette and Grandcourt. Our task was to break off and take heavy toll of the many German counter-attacks and on the rebound to win, yard by yard, ground which made our position secure.

In the desperate strain of this fighting there was evidence that the superb German machine was beginning to creak and falter. Hitherto, its strength had lain in the automatic precision of its ordering. Now, since reserves had to be hastily collected from all quarters, there was some fumbling in the direction. Attacks made by half a dozen battalions collected from three divisions, battalions which had never before been brigaded together, were bound to lack the old vigour and cohesion. Units lost direction, staff-work was imperfect, and what should have been a hammer-blow became a loose scrimmage. A captured letter written by an officer of the German 19th Corps revealed a change from the perfect coordination of the first year of war. "The job of relieving yesterday was incredible. From Courcelette we relieved across the open. Our position, of course, was quite different to what we had been told. Our company alone relieved a full battalion though we were only told to relieve a company of fifty men weakened through casualties. Those we relieved had no idea where the enemy was, how far off he was, or if any of our own troops were in front of us. We got no idea of our supposed position till 6 o'clock this evening. The English were 400 metres away, the Windmill just over the hill. We shall have to look to it to-night not to get taken prisoners. We have no dug-outs; we dig a hole in the side of a shell-hole and lie and get rheumatism. We get nothing to eat and drink. Yesterday each man drew two bottles of water and three iron rations, and these must last till we are relieved. The ceaseless roar of the guns is driving us mad, and many of the men are knocked up." Much of this discomfort was, to be sure, the fate of any troops in an advanced position, but there seemed to be an uncertainty as to purpose and a confusion in staff-work from which the Allies were now free.

It was the fashion in the German Press, at this time, to compare the Picardy offensive of the Allies with the German attack on Verdun, very much to the advantage of the latter. The deduction was false. In every military aspect — in the extent of ground won, in the respective losses, in the accuracy and weight of artillery, in the quality of the infantry attacks, and in the precision of the generalship — the Verdun attack fell far short of the Picardy battle. The Verdun front, in its operative part, had been narrower than that of the Somme, but at least ten more enemy divisions had by the beginning of August been attracted to Picardy than had appeared between Avocourt and Vaux up to the end of April. The Crown Prince at Verdun speedily lost the initiative in any serious sense; on the Somme von Below never possessed it. There the enemy had to accept battle as the Allied will imposed it, and no counter-attack could for a moment divert the resolute Allied purpose.

We have spoken of the stamina of the British troops, which was never tried more hardly than in the close-quarters fighting in the ruined villages and desolated woods of the German second position. No small part of it was due to the quality of the officers. When our great armies were improvised, the current fear was that a sufficient number of trained officers could not be provided to lead them. But the fear was groundless. The typical public-school boy proved a born leader of men. His good humour and *camaraderie*, his high sense of duty, his personal gallantry were the qualities most needed in the long months of trench warfare. When the advance came he was equal to the occasion. Much of the fighting was in small units, and the dash and intrepidity of men who a little before had been schoolboys was a notable asset in this struggle of sheer human quality. The younger officers sacrificed themselves freely, and it was the names of platoon commanders that filled most of the casualty lists.

Men fell who promised to win the highest distinction in civilian life. Many died, who were of the stuff from which the future leaders of the British Army would have been drawn. Such, to name one conspicuous instance, was Major William Congreve, who fell at Delville Wood at the age of twenty-five, having in two years of war already proved that he possessed the mind and character of a great soldier. It was a heavy price we paid, but who shall say that it was not well paid — not only in military results, but in the proof to our country and to the world that our officers were worthy of our men, and that they realised to the full the pride and duty of leadership? In an address given in the spring to a school for young officers, one of the most brilliant — and one of the youngest — of British generals told his hearers: "Remember that, though we are officers and the men are privates, still *we are all comrades* in the great dangers and the great struggle; make the men feel that you realise this comradeship and *love it*...Do not overlook the fact that the British soldier has a great soul, and can appreciate what courage, honour, patriotism and self-sacrifice mean." That lesson had been well and truly learned, and the result was "one equal temper of heroic minds" in all ranks of the British Army.

The list of Victoria Crosses can never be an adequate record of gallantry; it is no more than a sample of what in less conspicuous form was found everywhere in the battle. But in that short list there are exploits of courage and sacrifice which have never been surpassed. Major Loudoun-Shand, of the Yorkshires, fell mortally wounded while leading his men over the parapets, but he insisted on being propped up in a trench and encouraged his battalion till he died. Lieutenant Cather, of the Royal Irish Fusiliers, died while bringing in wounded from no-man's-land and carrying water to those who could not be moved, in full view and under the direct fire of the enemy.

Second-Lieutenant Simpson Bell, of the Yorkshires, found his company enfiladed, during an attack, by a German machine-gun. Of his own initiative he crept with a corporal and a private up a communication trench, crossed the open, and destroyed the machine-gun and its gunners, thereby saving many lives and ensuring the success of the British movement. A similar exploit was that of Company-Sergeant-Major Carter, of the Royal Sussex, who fell in the attempt. Corporal Sanders, of the West Yorkshires, found himself cut off in the enemy line with a party of thirty men. For two days he held the post, without food or water, and beat off German attacks, till relief came and he brought back his remnant of nineteen to our lines. Private Miller, of the Royal Lancashires, was sent through a heavy *barrage* with a message to which a reply was urgently wanted. Almost at once he was shot through the back, the bullet coming out in front. "In spite of this, with heroic courage and self-sacrifice, he compressed with his hand the gaping wound in his abdomen, delivered his message, staggered back with the answer, and fell at the feet of the officer to whom he delivered it. He gave his life with a supreme devotion to duty." Private Short, of the Yorkshires, was foremost in a bombing attack and refused to go back though severely wounded.

Finally his leg was shattered by a shell, but as he lay dying he was adjusting detonators and straightening bomb-pins for his comrades. "For the last eleven months he had always volunteered for dangerous enterprises, and has always set a magnificent example of bravery and devotion to duty."

Officers sacrificed themselves for their men, and men gave their lives for their officers. Private Veale, of the Devons, went out to look for an officer and found him among-standing corn fifty yards from the enemy. He dragged him to a shell hole and went back for water. Then, after vain efforts to bring him in, he went out with a party at dusk, and while they did their work he kept off an enemy patrol with a Lewis gun. Private Turrall, of the Worcesters, when an officer was badly wounded in a bombing attack which had been compelled to fall back, stayed with him for three hours under continuous fire, completely surrounded by the enemy. When a counter-attack made it possible he carried the officer back to our lines.

Private Quigg, of the Royal Irish Rifles, went out seven times under heavy machine-gun and shell fire to look for a lost platoon-commander, and for seven hours laboured to bring in wounded. Another type of service was that of Drummer Ritchie, of the Seaforths, who stood on the parapet of an enemy trench sounding the charge to rally men of various units who had lost their leaders and were beginning to retire.

And, perhaps the finest of all, there was Private McFadzean, of the Royal Irish Rifles, who, while opening a box of bombs before an attack, let the box slip so that two of the safety pins fell out. Like Lieutenant Smith, of the East Lancashires, at Gallipoli, he flung himself on the bombs, and the explosion, which blew him to pieces, only injured one other man. "He well knew the danger, being himself a bomber, but without a minute's hesitation he gave his life for his comrades." The General was right when he told his hearers that the British soldier has a great soul.

*

The French by the second week of August had carried, as we have seen, all the German third position south of the Somme. On Saturday, August 12th, after preparatory reconnaissances, they assaulted the third line north of the river from the east of Hardecourt to opposite Buscourt. It was a superbly organised assault, which on a front of over four miles swept away the enemy trenches and redoubts to an average depth of three-quarters of a mile. They entered the cemetery of Maurepas and the southern slopes of Hill 109 on the

Maurepas-Clery road, and reached the saddle west of Clery village. By the evening over 1,000 prisoners were in their hands. Four days later, on Wednesday, August 16th, they pushed their left flank — there adjoining the British — north of Maurepas, taking a mile of trenches, and south of that village took all the enemy line on a front of a mile and a quarter. Except for a few inconsiderable sections the enemy third position opposite the French had gone.

The British to the north were not yet ready for their grand assault. They had the more difficult ground, and for six weeks had been steadily fighting up hill. At points they had reached the watershed, but they had not won enough of the high ground to give them positions against the German third line on the reverse slopes. The following week was therefore a tale of slow progress to the rim of the plateau, around Pozières, High Wood, and Guillemont. Each day saw something gained by hard fighting. On Sunday, the 13th, it was a section of trench N.W. of Pozières, and another between Bazentin-le-Petit and Martinpuich. On Tuesday it was ground close to Mouquet Farm. On Wednesday it was the west and southwest environs of Guillemont and a 300-yards advance at High Wood. On Thursday there was progress northwest of

Bazentin-le-Petit towards Martinpuich and between Ginchy and Guillemont.

On Friday afternoon, August 18th, came the next combined attack. There was a steady pressure everywhere from Thiepval to the Somme. The advance began at 5 o'clock in the afternoon, in fantastic weather, with bursts of hot sunshine followed by thunderstorms and flights of rainbows. South of Thiepval, in the old German first line, was a strong work, the Leipzig Redoubt, into which we had already bitten. It was such a stronghold as we had seen at Beaumont Hamel, a nest of deep dug-outs and subterranean galleries, well stocked with machine-guns. As our front moved east to Pozières and Contalmaison we had neglected this corner, which had gradually become the apex of a sharp salient. It was garrisoned by Prussians of the 29th Regiment, who were confident in the impregnability of their refuge. They led an easy life, while their confederates on the crest were crowding in improvised trenches under our shelling. Those not on duty slept peacefully in their bunks at night, and played cards in the deep shelters.

On Friday afternoon, after a sharp and sudden artillery preparation, two British battalions rushed the redoubt. We had learned by this time how to deal with the German machine-guns. Many of the garrison fought stubbornly to the end; others we smoked out and rounded up like the occupants of a gambling-house surprised by the police. Six officers and a hundred and seventy men surrendered in a body. In all, some two thousand Germans were caught in this trap by numbers less than their own. There was no chance of a counter-stroke, for we got our machine-guns in position at once and our artillery caught every enemy attempt in the open.

Elsewhere on the front there was hard fighting. In the centre we pushed close to Martinpuich, and from High Wood southward we advanced our lines on a frontage of more than two miles for a distance varying from 200 to 600 yards. We took the stone quarry on the edge of Guillemont after a hand-to-hand struggle of several hours. Meantime the French carried the greater part of Maurepas village, and the place called Calvary Hill to the southeast. This last was a great feat of arms, for they had against them a fresh division of the Prussian Guards, which had seen no serious action for many months.

We were now fighting on the watershed. At Thiepval we held the ridge that overlooked it from the southeast. We held all the high ground north of Pozières, which gave us a clear view of the country towards Bapaume, and our lines lay 300 yards beyond the Windmill. We had all the west side of High Wood and the ground between it and the Albert-Bapaume road. We were half-way between Longueval and Ginchy, and our pincers encircled Guillemont. At last we were in position over against, and in direct view of, the German third line.

*

The next week was occupied in repelling German attempts to recover lost ground and in efforts to sharpen still further the Thiepval salient and to capture Guillemont. Thiepval, it should be remembered, was a point in the old German first line on the left flank of the great breach, and Guillemont was the one big position still untaken in the German second line. On Sunday, the 20th, the Germans shelled our front heavily and at about noon attacked our new lines on the western side of High Wood. They reached a portion of our trenches, but were immediately driven out by our infantry. Next day, at High Wood and at Mouquet Farm, there were frequent bombing attacks which came to nothing. On Tuesday, August 21st, we advanced steadily on our left, pushing our line to the very edge of what was once Mouquet Farm as well as to the northeast of it, and closing in to within 1,000 yards of Thiepval.

The weather had become clearer, and our counter-battery work silenced some of the enemy's guns, while our aircraft fought many battles. We lost no single machine, but four enemy airplanes were destroyed and many others driven to the ground in a damaged condition. A sentence in a captured letter paid a tribute to the efficiency of the British airmen: "The airmen circle over us and try to do damage, but only enemy ones, for a German airman will not try to come near. Behind the front there is a great crowd of them, but here not one makes his appearance."

Throughout the whole battle there was no question which side possessed the ascendancy in the air. Here is the record of the doings of one flight-lieutenant, who encountered a detachment of twelve German machines. "He dived in among them, firing one drum. The formation was broken up. Lieutenant — then got under the nearest machine and fired one drum at 15 yards under the pilot's seat, causing the machine to plunge to earth southeast of Bapaume. Shortly afterwards some more hostile aeroplanes came up in formation. Lieutenant — attacked one, which went down and landed in a gap between the woods. Several other machines were engaged with indecisive results, and, having expended all his ammunition, Lieutenant — returned." This was on September 1st. Lieutenant — took the day's work as calmly as if he had been shooting partridges.

On Wednesday night and Thursday morning a very severe counter-attack on our position at Guillemont, pressed with great determination, failed to win any ground. That afternoon, August 24th, we advanced nearer Thiepval, coming, at one point, within 500 yards of the place. In the evening, at five o'clock, the French carried Maurepas and pushed their right on to the Combles railway. Next day the French success enabled us to join up with our Allies southeast of Guillemont, where our pincers were now beginning to grip hard.

The following week was one of slow and steady progress. We cleared the ground immediately north of Delville Wood by a dashing charge of the Rifle Brigade. The most satisfactory feature of these days was the frequency of the German counter-attacks and their utter failure. On August 26th, for example, troops of the Prussian Guard, after a heavy bombardment, attacked south of Thiepval village and were completely repulsed by the Wiltshire and Worcestershire battalions holding that front. One incident of the day deserves record. A despatch runner was sent back with a message to the rear, which he reached safely. He started back, came unscathed through the German *barrage*, but in the general ruin of the trench lines failed to find the place he had left. He wandered on and on till he reached something that looked like his old trench, and was just about to enter it when he found it packed with Germans. He immediately jumped to the conclusion that a counter-attack was about to be launched, and, slipping back, managed to reach our own lines, where he told the news. In a minute or two our artillery got on to the spot, and the counter-attack of the Prussian Guard was annihilated before it began. On Thursday evening, August 31st, five violent and futile assaults were made on our front between High Wood and Ginchy. It looked as if the enemy was trying in vain to anticipate the next great stage of our offensive which was now imminent.

*

On Sunday, September 3rd, the whole Allied front pressed forward. In the early morning the Australians attacked on the extreme left — near Mouquet Farm and towards Thiepval. There they encountered some of the Guard reserves, and took several hundred prisoners. They carried various strong positions, won ground east of Mouquet Farm, and still further narrowed the Thiepval salient. The British right, attacking in the afternoon, swept through Guillemont to the sunken road — 500 yards to the east. They captured Ginchy also, but were forced later in the day to relinquish the eastern part of that village. Further south they fought their way to the east of Falfemont Farm, where they joined hands with the triumphant French. For the French on that day had marched steadily from victory to victory. Shortly after noon, on a 3¾ miles front between Maurepas and the Somme, they had attacked after an intense artillery preparation. They carried the villages of Le Forest and Clèry, and north of the former place won the German lines to the outskirts of Combles.

As the bloody angle south of Beaumont Hamel will be for ever associated with the Ulster Division, so Guillemont was a triumph for the troops of southern and western Ireland. The men of Munster, Leinster, and Connaught broke through the intricate defences of the enemy as a torrent sweeps down rubble. The place was one of the strongest of all the many fortified villages in the German line, and its capture was the most important achievement of the British since the taking of Pozières. It was the last uncaptured point in the old German second position between Mouquet Farm and the junction with the French. It was most resolutely defended, since, being close to the point of junction, it compelled a hiatus in the advance of the Allied front. With its fall the work of two years was swept away, and in the whole section the enemy were now in new and improvised positions. But the advance was only beginning. On Monday, September 4th, all enemy counterattacks were beaten off, and further ground won by the British near Falfemont Farm. That night, in a torrent of rain, our men pressed on, and before midday on Tuesday, September 5th, they were nearly a mile east of Guillemont and well into Leuze Wood. By that evening the whole of the wood was taken, and the British were less than 1,000 yards from the town of Combles, on which the French were pressing in on the south. Meantime, about two in the afternoon, a new French army came into action south of the Somme on a front of a dozen miles from Barleux to south of Chaulnes. At a bound it carried the whole of the German first position from Vermandovillers to Chilly, a front of nearly 3 miles, and took some 3,000 unwounded prisoners. Next day the French pressed on both north and south of the river, and in the former area reached the west end of the Anderlu Wood, carried the Hôpital Farm, the Rainette Wood, part of the Marrière Wood, the ridge on which runs the road from Bouchavesnes to Clèry, and the village of Omiécourt.

From Wednesday, September 6th, to the night of Friday, the 8th, the Germans strove in vain to win back what they had lost. On the whole 30 miles from Thiepval to Chilly there were violent counter-attacks which had no success. The Allied artillery broke up the massed infantry in most cases long before they reached our trenches. On Saturday, September 9th, the same Irish regiments which had won Guillemont carried Ginchy. The Allied front was now in a symmetrical line, and everywhere on the highest ground. Combles was held in a tight clutch, and the French new army was within 800 yards of Chaulnes Station, and was holding 2½ miles of the Chaulnes-Roye railway, thereby cutting the chief German line of lateral communication. The first objective which the Allies had set before themselves on July 1st had been amply won.

CHAPTER FOUR –
CONCLUSION TO FIRST PHASE

This narrative reaches its conclusion at the moment when the British had made good the old German second position and had won the crest of the uplands — when the French in their section had advanced almost to the gates of Peronne and their new army on the right had begun to widen the breach. That moment was in a very real sense the end of a phase, the first and perhaps the most critical phase of the great Western offensive. A man may have saved money so that he can face the beginnings of adversity with cheerfulness; but if the stress continues, his money will come to an end, and he will be no better than his fellows in misfortune. The immense fortifications of her main position represented for Germany the accumulated capital of two years. She had raised these defences when she was stronger than her adversaries in guns and in men. Now she was weaker, and her capital was gone. Thenceforth the campaign entered upon a new stage, and the first stage, which in strict terms we can call the Battle of the Somme, had ended in an Allied victory.

By what test are we to judge the result of a battle in modern war? In the old days of open fighting there was little room for doubt, since the retreat or rout or envelopment of the beaten army was too clear for argument. To-day, when the total battle front is 2,000 miles, such easy proofs are lacking; but the principle remains the same. A battle is final when it ends in the destruction of the enemy's fighting strength. A battle is won — and it may be decisively won — when it results in achieving the strategic purpose of one of the combatants, provided that purpose is, on military grounds, a wise one. Hence the amount of territory occupied and the number of important points captured are not necessarily sound criteria at all. If they were, the German overrunning of Poland would have been a great victory, when, as a matter of fact, it was a disastrous failure. Von Hindenburg sought to destroy the Russian army, and the Russian army declined the honour. The success or defeat of a strategic purpose, that is the sole test. Judging by this, Tannenberg was a victory for Germany, the Marne for France, and the first battle of Ypres for Britain. The battle of the Somme was no less a victory, since it achieved the Allied purpose and frustrated that of the enemy.

The German purpose we know. It was to hold their ground, to maintain the mighty defences on which they had spent so many months of labour, to beat off the attack at whatever cost. The Allied aim must be clearly understood. It was not to recover so many square miles of France; it was not to take Bapaume or Peronne or St. Quentin; it was not even in the strict sense to carry this or that position. All these things were subsidiary and would follow in due course, provided the main purpose succeeded. That purpose was simply to exercise a steady and continued pressure on a certain section of the enemy's front.

For nearly two years the world has been full of theories as to the possibility of breaking the German line. It is many months since critics pointed out the futility of piercing that line on too narrow a front, since all that was produced thereby was an awkward salient. It was clear that any breach must be made on a wide front, which would allow the attacking wedge to manoeuvre in the gap, and prevent reinforcements from coming up quickly enough to reconstitute the line behind. But this view took too little account of the strength of the German fortifications. No doubt a breach could be made; but its making would be desperately costly, for no bombardment could destroy all the defensive lines, and infantry in the attack would be somewhere or other faced with unbroken wire and unshaken parapets. Gradually it was accepted that an attack should proceed by stages, with, as a prelude to each, a complete artillery preparation, and that, since the struggle must be long drawn out, fresh troops should be used at each stage.

These were the tactics of the Germans at Verdun, and they were obviously right. Why, then, did the attack on Verdun fail? In the first place, because after the first week the assault became spasmodic and the great plan fell to pieces. Infantry were used wastefully in hopeless rushes. The pressure was relaxed for days on end, and the defence was allowed to reorganise itself. The second reason, of which the first was a consequence, was that Germany, after the initial onslaught, had not the necessary superiority either in numbers or *moral* or guns. At the Somme the Allies did not relax their pressure, and their strength was such that they could keep it continuously at the highest power.

A strategical problem is not, as a rule, capable of being presented in a simple metaphor, but we may say that the huge German salient in the West was like an elastic band drawn very tight. Each part has lost elasticity, and may be severed by friction, which would do little harm to the band if less tautly stretched. That represents one element in the situation. Another aspect may be suggested by the metaphor of a sea-dyke of stone in a flat country where all stone must be imported. The waters crumble the wall in one section, and all free reserves of stone are used to strengthen that part. But the crumbling goes on, and to fill the breach stones are brought from other sections of the dyke. Some day there must come an hour when the sea will wash through the old breach, and a great length of the weakened dyke will follow in the cataclysm.

In the first two months of the Somme battle some forty-four German divisions — more than ever appeared at Verdun — were drawn into the whirlpool, and many were sent in twice. They represented the *élite* of the German army. The Allies have taken heavy toll of these; some 50,000 unwounded prisoners are in their hands; many German counter-attacks have been caught in our *barrage* and destroyed; and every line of trench taken has meant many German dead. They have drawn into the battle and gravely depleted the surplus manpower of the enemy. They have done more: they have struck a shattering blow at his *moral*. For two years the German behind the shelter of his trench-works and the great engine of his artillery fought with comparatively little cost against opponents far less well equipped. To-day the shoe is on the other foot, and he is coming to know what the British learned at Ypres and the French in the Artois — what it feels like to be bombarded out of existence and to cling to shell holes and the ruins of trenches under a pitiless fire. It is a new thing in his experience, and it has taken the heart out of men who under other conditions fought with skill and courage. Further, the Allies have dislocated his whole military machine. Their ceaseless pressure is crippling his Staff work and confusing the organisation of which he justly boasted. To-day Germany is the Allies' inferior. The weaker side in every element which constitutes the strength of an army, she is subject in the field to the Allies' will.

Now it is a law of life and of war that in such struggles the power of the stronger grows *pari passu* with the weakness of the less strong. That is the security for the continuance of the Allied plan. Repeatedly in the last two months Germany announced that the offensive on the Somme must slacken; repeatedly she declared that it had ceased; but the beginning of September saw the assault as sternly maintained as in the first days of July. Like some harsh and remorseless chemical the waxing Allied energy is eating into the waning German mass. There is thought and care in the plan, and that resolution which is so strong that it can dare to be patient. The guarantee of the continuity of the Allied effort is its orderly and accurate progress. The heroic dash may fail and be shattered by the counter-attack, but this sure and methodical pressure is as resistless as the forces of Nature. It is attrition, but attrition in the acute form — not like the slow erosion of cliffs by the sea, but like the steady crumbling of a mountain to which hydraulic engineers have applied a mighty head of water. The time must come when the far-flung German lines will be exhausted by the strain and will seek to retire. In that falling back, with the Allies all round the salient at their throats, may be fought the decisive action of the war.

*

A sketch of the main features of a great action is like the rough outline of a picture before the artist has added the colours and the proportions of life. It cannot even hint at the rich human quality of it all, the staunch brotherhood in arms, the faithfulness, the cheerful sacrifice, the fortitude, any more than it can portray the terror and suffering. But it is well to realise that this battle, unparalleled in its magnitude and gravity, was also unique in another circumstance. It was the effort of the whole British nation, and an effort made of each man's free will. Her armies were not a separate caste, whose doings the ordinary citizen watched with interest and excitement, but with a certain detachment, as those of friendly gladiators hired for a purpose foreign to the decent routine of his life. They were composed of the ordinary citizen himself. The Army was the people. Not a class or profession or trade but had sent its tens of thousands to the ranks, and scarcely a British home but had losses to mourn. Those fighting men had come willingly to the task, because their own interest and happiness were become one with their country's victory. Having willed the end, they willed also the means, and showed themselves gluttons for the full rigour of service. One old doubt has been resolved. Could free men show the highest discipline? Was that acme of organisation which a conquering army demands compatible with a true democracy? "It has long been a grave question," said Abraham Lincoln, nearly sixty years ago, "whether any Government, not too strong for the liberties of its people, can be strong enough to maintain its existence in great emergencies." That riddle is now nobly answered. No great thing is achieved without a price, and on the Somme fell the very flower of Britain, the straightest of limb, the keenest of brain, the most eager of spirit. In such a mourning each man thinks first of his friends. Each of us has seen his crowded circle become like the stalls of a theatre at an unpopular play, Each has suddenly found the world of time strangely empty and eternity strangely thronged. To look back upon the gallant procession of those who offered their all and had their gift accepted, is to know exultation as well as sorrow. The young men who died almost before they had looked on the world, the makers and the doers who left their tasks unfinished, were greater in their deaths than in their lives. They builded better than they knew, for the sum of their imperfections was made perfect, and out of loss they won for their country and mankind an enduring gain. Their memory will abide so long as men are found to set honour before ease, and a nation lives not for its ledgers alone but for some purpose of virtue. They have become, in the fancy of Henry Vaughan, the shining spires of that City to which we travel.

CHAPTER FIVE –
THE SEPTEMBER CAMPAIGN

The capture of Guillemont on September 3rd meant the end of the German second position on the whole front between Thiepval and Estrées. The Allies were faced with a new problem, to understand which it is necessary to consider the nature of the defences still before them and the peculiar configuration of the country.

The advance of July 1st had carried the first enemy lines on a broad front, but the failure of the attack between Gommecourt and Thiepval had made the breach eight miles less than the original plan. The advance of July 14th gave us the second line on a still narrower front — from Bazentin le Petit to Longueval. The danger now was that the Allied thrust, if continued, might show a rapidly narrowing wedge which would result in the formation of a sharp and precarious salient. Accordingly Sir Douglas Haig broadened the breach by striking out to left and right, capturing first Pozières and the high ground at Mouquet Farm, and then — on his other flank — Guillemont and Ginchy. These successes made the gap in the second position some seven miles wide, and brought the British front in most places to the highest ground, from which direct observation was obtainable over the lower slopes and valley pockets to the east. We did not yet hold the complete crown of the ridge, though at Mouquet Farm and at High Wood we had positions which no superior height commanded.

The German third position had at the beginning of the battle been only in embryo. Before the attack of July 14th it had been more or less completed, and by the beginning of September it had been greatly elaborated and a fourth position prepared behind it. It was based on a string of fortified villages which lie on the reverse slopes of the main ridge — Courcelette, Martinpuich, Flers, Lesboeufs, and Morval. Behind it was an intermediate line, with Le Sars, Eaucourt l'Abbaye, and Gueudecourt as strong positions in it; and further back a fourth position, which lay just west of the Bapaume-Peronne road, covering the villages of Sailly-Saillisel and Le Transloy.

This was the line protecting Bapaume; the next position, at this moment only roughly sketched out, lay well to the east of that town.

Since the battle began the Germans had, up to the second week in September, brought 61 Divisions into action in the Somme area; 7 had been refitted and sent in again; on September 14th they were holding the line with 15 Divisions — which gives us 53 as the number which had been used up. The German losses throughout had been high. The French casualties had been singularly light — for they had fought economically under close cover of their guns, and had had, on the whole, the easier tactical problem to face. The British losses had been, beyond doubt, lower than those of the enemy, and our most conspicuous successes, such as the advance of July 1st south of Thiepval and the action of July 14th, had been achieved at a comparatively small cost. Our main casualties arose from the failure north of Thiepval on the first day, and the taking of desperately defended and almost impregnable positions like Delville Wood and Guillemont. In the ten weeks' battle the enemy had shown many ups and downs of strength. At one moment his whole front would appear to be crumbling; at another the arrival of fresh batteries from Verdun and new troops would solidify his line. The effort had strained his capacity to its full. He had revived the old

First Army — which had been in abeyance since the preceding spring — and given it to von Below north of the Somme, while the Second Army, now under von Gallwitz, held the front south of the river. He had placed the Crown Prince of Bavaria, commanding the Sixth Army, in charge of the sector comprising his own and the First and Second Armies, He had followed the British plan of departing from the old Corps system and creating groups — through which a large number of Divisions, drawn from many Corps, were successively passed. He had used in his defence the best fighting material he possessed. During those ten weeks almost all the most famous German units had appeared on the Somme — the cream of the Bavarian troops, the Fifth Brandenburgers, and every single Division of the Guard and Guard Reserve Corps.

*

In the early days of September there was evidence that the enemy was in no very happy condition. The loss of Ginchy and Guillemont had enabled the British to come into line with the left wing of Fayolle's great advance, while the fall of certain vital positions on the

Thiepval Ridge gave us observation over a great space of country and threatened Thiepval — which was the pivot of all the German defence in the northern section of the battle-ground. The Allied front north of the Somme had the river as a defensive flank on its right, and might presently have the Ancre to fill the same part on its left. Hence the situation was ripe for a further thrust which, if successful, might give our advance a new orientation. If the German third line could be carried it might be possible to strike out on the flanks, repeating on a far greater scale the practice already followed. Bapaume itself was not the objective, but a thrust northeastward across the upper Ancre, which might get behind the great slab of unbroken enemy positions from Thiepval northwards. That would be the ultimate reward of a complete success; in the meantime our task was to break through the enemy's third line and test his powers of resistance.

It seemed a propitious moment for a concerted blow. The situation on the whole front was good. Fayolie's left wing had won conspicuous successes and had their spirits high, while Micheler was moving his pincers towards Chaulnes and playing havoc with the main German lateral communications. Elsewhere in Europe things went well for the Allies. On August

28th Rumania had entered the war and her troops were pouring into Transylvania. As it happened, it was a premature and fruitless movement, but it compelled Germany to take instant steps to meet the menace. There had been important changes in the German Higher commands, and it might reasonably be assumed that von Hindenburg and von Ludendorff were not yet quite at ease in the saddle. Brussilov was still pinning down the Austro-German forces on the Russian front and Sarrail had just begun his serious offensive in the Balkans. In the event of a real *débâcle* in the West the enemy might be hard pressed to find the men to fill the breach.

Every action, it should be remembered, is a packet of surprises. There is an immediate local objective, but on success any one of twenty consequences may follow. The wise commander cannot count on any of these consequences, but he must not neglect them in his calculations. If the gods send him good fortune he must be ready to take it, and he naturally chooses a season when the gods seem propitious.

On Tuesday, September 12th, a comprehensive bombardment began all along the British front from Thiepval to Ginchy. The whole of Sir Henry Rawlinson's Fourth Army was destined for the attack, as well as the right Corps — the First Canadian — of the Fifth Army, while on the left of the battle to another Division was allotted a preliminary attack, which was partly in the nature of a feint and partly a necessary preparatory step. The immediate objective of the different units must be clearly noted. On the left of the main front one Canadian Division was directed against Courcelette. On their right a Division of the New Army — that Scottish Division which had won high honour at Loos — had for its task to clear the remains of the old Switch Line and encircle Martinpuich, but not — on the first day at any rate — to attempt the capture of what was believed to be a most formidable stronghold. Going south, two Territorial Divisions — Northumbrian and London — had to clear High Wood. On their right the New Zealanders had Flers as their objective, while two Divisions of the New Army had to make good the ground east and north of Delville Wood. Next to them the Guards and a Division of the old Regulars were to move northeast from Ginchy against Lesboeufs and Morval, while on the extreme right of the British front another Division of London Territorials were to carry Bouleaux Wood and form a defensive flank.

The forces to be used in the new advance were

for the most part fresh. The Guards had not been in action since Loos the previous September, the Canadians were new to the Somme area, while it was the first experience of the New Zealanders on the Western Front. Two of the Divisions had been some considerable time already in the front trenches, but the others had been brought up for the purpose only a few days before. All the troops were of the best quality, and had a proud record behind them. More perhaps than any other part of the battle this was an action of the British *corps d'élite*.

In this stage, too, a new weapon was to be used. The "tanks," officially known as "Machine Gun Corps, Heavy Section," had come out from home some time before and had been parked in secluded spots at the back of the front. The world is now familiar with descriptions and pictures of those strange machines, which, shaped like monstrous toads, crawled imperturbably over wire and parapets, butted down houses, shouldered trees aside, and humped themselves over the stoutest walls. They were an experiment which could only be proved in practice, and the design in using them at this stage was principally to find out their weak points, so as to perfect their mechanism for the future. Their main tactical purpose was to clear out redoubts and nests of machine-guns which, as we had found to our sorrow at Loos, might hang up the most resolute troops. For this object they must precede the infantry attack, and the task of assembling them before the parapets were crossed was fraught with difficulty, for they were neither silent nor inconspicuous. The things had been kept a profound secret, and until the very eve of the advance few in the British Army had even heard of them. On September 14th, the day before our attack, some of them were seen by German aeroplanes, and the German troops were warned that the British had some strange new engine. Rumours also seem to have reached Germany five or six weeks earlier, for orders had been issued to supply the soldiers with a special kind of armour-piercing bullet. But as to the real nature of the device the Germans had no inkling.

They had not grasped the principle, and it is doubtful if they have grasped it yet.

*

On the night of Thursday, the 14th, the Fifth Army carried out their preliminary task. On a front of a thousand yards southeast of Thiepval a Brigade of the New Army stormed the Hohenzollern Trench and the strong redoubt which the Germans called the "Wunderwerk," taking many prisoners and themselves losing little. The fame of this enterprise has been somewhat obscured by the great advance which followed, but it was a most workmanlike and skilful performance, and it had a real effect on the subsequent battle. It deceived the enemy as to the exact terrain of the main assault, and it caused him to launch a counterattack in an area which was part of the principal battle-ground, with the result that our left wing, after checking his attack, was able to catch him on the rebound.

The morning of Friday, September 15th, was perfect autumn weather with a light mist filling the hollows and shrouding the slopes. At 6 a.m. the British bombardment, which had now lasted for three days, rose to the fury of hurricane fire. The enemy had a thousand guns of all calibres massed against us, and his defences consisted of a triple line of entrenchments and a series of advanced posts manned by machine-guns. Our earlier bombardment had cut his wire and destroyed many of his trenches, besides hampering greatly his bringing up of men, rations, and shells. The final twenty minutes of intense fire, slowly creeping forward with our infantry close under its shadow, pinned him to his positions and interfered with his counter-barrage. To an observer it seemed that the deafening crescendo all round the horizon was wholly British.

At twenty minutes past six our men crossed the parapets and moved forward methodically towards the enemy. The Germans, manning their trenches as our guns lengthened, saw through the thin mist inhuman shapes crawling towards them, things like gigantic slugs, spitting fire from their mottled sides. They had been warned of a new weapon, but what mortal weapon was this terror that walked by day? And ere they could collect their dazed wits the British bayonets were upon them.

On the left and centre the attack was instantly successful. The Canadians, after beating off the German counter-attack, carried Courcelette in the afternoon. In this advance French-Canadian troops played a distinguished part in winning back some miles of French soil for their ancient Motherland. On their right the Scottish Division, which had already been six weeks in line, performed something more than the part allotted it. The capture of Martinpuich was not part of the programme of the day's operations, but the Scots pushed east and west of the village, and at a quarter past five in the evening had the place in their hands. Further south there was fierce fighting in the old cockpit of High Wood. It was two months since we had first effected an entrance into its ill-omened shades, but we had been forced back, and for long had to be content with its southern corner. The strong German third one — which ran across its northern half on the very crest of the ridge — and the endless craters and machine-gun redoubts made it a desperate nut to crack. We had pushed out horns to east and west of it, but the northern stronghold in the wood itself had defied all our efforts. It was held on that day by troops of the 2nd Bavarian Corps, and the German ranks have shown no better fighting stuff. Our first attack failed, but on a second attempt the London Territorials — a little after noon — swept the place clear, though not without heavy losses.

Beyond them the New Zealand Division, with a New Army Division on its right, carried the Switch line and took Flers with little trouble. They were preceded by a tank, which waddled complacently up the main street of the village, with the enemy's bullets rattling harmlessly off its sides, followed by cheering and laughing British troops. Further south we advanced our front for nearly a mile and a half. A light Division of the New Army, debouching from Delville Wood, cleared Mystery Corner on its eastern side before the general attack began, and then with splendid *élan* pushed forward north of Ginchy in the direction of Lesboeufs.

Only on the right wing was the tale of success incomplete. Ginchy, it will be remembered, had been carried by Irish troops on September 9th, but its environs were not yet fully cleared, and the enemy held the formidable point known as the Quadrilateral. This was situated about 700 yards east of Ginchy at a bend of the Morval road, where it passed through a deep wooded ravine. One of the old Regular Divisions was directed against it, with the Guards on their left and the London Territorials on their right. The business of the last-named was to carry Bouleaux Wood and form a defensive flank north of Combles, while the Guards were to advance from Ginchy on Lesboeufs. But the strength of the Quadrilateral foiled the plan. The Londoners did indeed enter Bouleaux Wood, but the Division on their left was fatally hung up in front of the Quadrilateral, and this in turn exposed the right flank of the Guards. The Guards Brigades advanced, as they have always advanced, with perfect discipline and courage. But both their flanks were enfiladed; the sunken road in front of them was strongly held by machine-guns; they somewhat lost direction; and, in consequence, no part of our right attack gained its full objective. There and in High Wood we incurred most of the casualties of the day. The check was the more regrettable since complete success in this area was tactically more important than elsewhere.

But after all deductions are made the day's results were in a high degree satisfactory. It was the most effective blow yet dealt at the enemy by British troops. It gave us not only the high ground between Thiepval and the Combles Valley, but placed us well down the forward slopes. "The damage to the enemy's *moral*," says the official summary, "is probably of greater consequence than the seizure of dominating positions and the capture of between four and five thousand prisoners." Three famous Bavarian Divisions had been engaged and completely shattered, and the whole enemy front thrown into a state of disorder. The tanks had, for a new experiment, done wonders. Some of them broke down on the way up, and of the twenty-four which crossed the German lines, seven came to grief early in the day. The remaining seventeen did brilliant service, some squatting on enemy trenches and clearing them by machine-gun fire, some flattening out uncut wire, others destroying machine-gun nests and redoubts or strong points like the sugar factory at Courcelette. But their moral effect was greater than the material damage they wrought. The sight of those deliberate impersonal engines ruthlessly grinding down the most cherished defences put something like panic into troops who had always prided themselves upon the superior merit of their own fighting "machine." Beyond doubt, too, the presence of the tanks added greatly to the zeal and confidence of our assaulting infantry. An element of sheer comedy was introduced into the grim business of war, and comedy is dear to the heart of the British soldier. The crews of the tanks — which they called His Majesty's Landships — seemed to have acquired some of the light-heartedness of the British sailor. Penned up in a narrow stuffy space, condemned to a form of motion compared with which that of the queasiest vessel is stable, and at the mercy of unknown perils, these adventurers faced their task with the zest of a boy on holiday. With infinite humour they described how the enemy had surrounded them when they were stuck, and had tried in vain to crack their shell, while they themselves sat laughing inside.

In the achievements of the day our aircraft nobly co-operated. They destroyed thirteen hostile machines and drove nine more in a broken condition to ground. They bombarded enemy headquarters and vital points on all his railway lines. They destroyed German kite balloons and so put out the eyes of the defence. They guided our artillery fire and they brought back frequent and accurate reports of every stage in the infantry advance. Moreover, they attacked both enemy artillery and infantry with their machine-gun fire from a low elevation. Such performances were a proof of that resolute and exalted spirit of the offensive which inspired all arms of the service. In the week of the action on the whole Somme battle-ground only fourteen enemy machines managed to cross our lines, while our aeroplanes made between two thousand and three thousand flights far behind the German front.

*

In the Guards' advance, among many other gallant and distinguished officers, there fell one whose death was, in a peculiar sense, a loss to his country and the future. Lieutenant Raymond Asquith, of the Grenadier Guards, the eldest son of the British Prime Minister, died while leading his men through the fatal enfilading fire from the corner of Ginchy village. In this war the gods have taken toll of every rank and class. Few generals and statesmen in the Allied nations but have had to mourn intimate bereavements, and De Castelnau has given three sons for his country. But the death of Raymond Asquith had a poignancy apart from his birth and position, and it may be permitted to one of his oldest friends to pay his tribute to a heroic memory.

A scholar of the ripe Elizabethan type, a brilliant wit, an accomplished poet, a sound lawyer — these things were borne lightly, for his greatness was not in his attainments but in himself. He had always a curious aloofness towards mere worldly success. He loved the things of the mind for their own sake — good books, good talk, the company of old friends — and the rewards of common ambition seemed to him too trivial for a man's care.

He was of the spending type in life, giving freely of the riches of his nature, but asking nothing in return. His carelessness of personal gain, his inability to trim or truckle, and his aloofness from the facile acquaintanceships of the modern world made him incomprehensible to many, and his high fastidiousness gave him a certain air of coldness. Most noble in presence and with every grace of voice and manner, he moved among men like a being of another race, scornfully detached from the vulgarities of the common struggle, and only his friends knew the warmth and loyalty of his soul.

At the outbreak of war he joined a Territorial battalion, from which he was later transferred to the Grenadiers. More than most men he hated the loud bellicosities of politics, and he had never done homage to the deities of the crowd. His critical sense made him chary of enthusiasm, and it was no sudden sentimental fervour that swept him into the Army. He saw his duty, and, though it meant the shattering of every taste and interest, he did it joyfully, and did it to the full. For a little he had a post on the Staff, but applied to be sent back to his battalion, since he wished no privileges. In the Guards he was extraordinarily happy, finding the same kind of light-hearted and high-spirited companionship which had made Oxford for him a place of delectable memories. He was an admirable battalion officer, and thought seriously of taking up the Army as his profession after the war — for he had all the qualities which go to make up a good soldier.

In our long roll of honour no nobler figure will find a place, He was a type of his country at its best — shy of rhetorical professions, austerely self-respecting, one who hid his devotion under a mask of indifference, and, when the hour came, revealed it only in deeds. Many gave their all for the cause, but few, if any, had so much to give. He loved his youth, and his youth has become eternal. Debonair and brilliant and brave, he is now part of that immortal England which knows not age or weariness or defeat.

*

Meanwhile the French had not been idle. On Wednesday, September 13th, two days before the British advance, Fayolle carried Bouchavesnes east of the Bapaume-Peronne road, taking over two thousand prisoners. He was now not three miles from the vital position of Mont St. Quentin — the key of Peronne — facing it across the little valley of the Tortille. Next day the French had the farm of Le Priez, southeast of Combles, and on the afternoon on Sunday, the 17th, south of the Somme their right wing carried the remainder of Vermandovillers and Berny, and the intervening ground around Deniécourt. The following day Deniécourt, with its strongly-fortified park, was captured. This gave them the whole of the Berny-

Deniécourt plateau, commanding the lower plateau where stood the villages of Ablaincourt and Pressoire, and menaced Barleux — the pivot of enemy resistance south of the river.

For the next week there was a lull in the main operations while the hammer was swung back for another blow. On the 16th the 45th German Reserve Division counter-attacked the Canadians at Courcelette, and the 6th Bavarian Division, newly arrived, struck at the New Zealanders at Flers. Both failed, and south of Combles the fresh troops of the German 18th Corps succeeded no better against the French. The most vigorous counter-strokes were those which the Canadians received, and which were repeated daily for nearly a week. Meantime, on Monday, the 18th, the Quadrilateral was carried — carried by the Regular Division which had been blocked by it three days before. It was not won without a heavy fight at close quarters, for the garrison resisted stoutly, but we closed in on it from all sides, and by the evening had pushed our front five hundred yards beyond it to the hollow before Morval.

The week was dull and cloudy, and from the Monday to the Wednesday it rained without ceasing. But by the Friday it had cleared, though the mornings were now thick with autumn haze, and we were able once more to get that direct observation and aerial reconnaissance which is an indispensable preliminary to a great attack. On Sunday, the 24th, our batteries opened again, this time against the uncaptured points in the German third line like Morval and Lesboeufs, against intermediate positions like Gueudecourt, and especially against Thiepval — which we now commanded from the east. On that day, too, our aircraft destroyed six enemy machines and drove three more to earth. The plan was for an attack by the Fourth Army on Monday, the 25th, with — on its left wing — small local objectives; but, on the right and centre, aiming at completing the captures which had been the ultimate objectives of the advance of the 15th. The following day the right wing of the Fifth Army would come into action, and it was hoped that from Thiepval to Combles the enemy would be driven back to his fourth line of defence, and our own front pushed up well within assaulting distance.

The hour of attack on the 25th was fixed at thirty-five minutes after noon. It was bright, cloudless weather, but the heat of the sun had lost its summer strength. That day saw an advance the most perfect yet made in any stage of the battle, for in almost every part of the field we won what we sought. The extreme left of the Third Corps was held up north of Courcelette, but its remaining two Divisions carried out the tasks assigned to them. So did the centre and left Divisions of the Fifteenth Corps, while part of the right Division managed to penetrate into Gueudecourt, but was compelled to retire owing to the supporting Brigade on its flank being checked by uncut wire. The Fourteenth Corps succeeded everywhere. The Guards, eager to avenge their sufferings of the week before, despite the heavy losses on their left, swept irresistibly upon Lesboeufs. South of them a Regular Division took Morval — the village on the height north of Combles which, with its subterranean quarries and elaborate trench system, was a most formidable stronghold. The London Territorials on their right formed a defensive flank facing south at Bouleaux Wood. Combles was now fairly between the pincers. It might have fallen that day, but the French attack on Frégicourt failed, though they carried the village of Rancourt on the Bapaume-Peronne road.

By the evening of the 25th the British had stormed an enemy front of six miles between Combles and Martinpuich to a depth of more than a mile. The fall of Morval gave them the last piece of uncaptured high ground on that backbone of ridge which runs from Thiepval through High Wood and Ginchy. The next day we reaped in full the fruit of these successes. The Division of the New Army which had entered Gueudecourt the day before, but had failed to maintain their ground, now captured the famous Gird Trench, assisted by a tank and an aeroplane — which attacked the enemy with machine-gun fire — and by the afternoon had the village in their hands. This Division was one which had suffered disaster at Loos a year before on that very day, and had, since the beginning of the Somme battle, shown that there is no more formidable antagonist than a British unit which has a score to pay off. It had already played a large part in the capture of Fricourt; it had cleared Mametz Wood, and it had taken Bazentin-le-Petit Wood on July 14th. It now crowned a brilliant record by the capture of Gueudecourt and an advance to within a mile of the German fourth position.

That day, too, the French took Frégicourt, and Combles fell. The enemy had evacuated it, and though great stores of material were taken in its catacombs, the number of prisoners was small.

Meantime, on the British left the success was not less conspicuous. Two Divisions of the New Army, advancing under the cover of our artillery barrage, had carried Thiepval. the northwest corner of Mouquet Farm and the Zollern Redoubt on the eastern crest. The German pivot had gone, the pivot which they had believed impregnable. So skilful was our barrage that our men were over the German parapets and into the dug-outs before machine-guns could be got up to repel them. Here the prisoners were numerous, for the attack was in the nature of a surprise.

On the evening of September 26th the Allied fortunes in the West had never looked brighter. The enemy was now on his fourth line, without the benefit of the high ground, and there was no chance of retrieving his disadvantages by observation from the air. Since July 1st the British alone had taken over twenty-six thousand prisoners, and had engaged thirty-eight German Divisions, the flower of the Army, of which twenty-nine had been withdrawn exhausted and broken. The enemy had been compelled to use up his reserves in repeated costly and futile counter-attacks without compelling the Allies to relax for one moment their steady and methodical pressure. Every part of the Armies of France and Britain had done gloriously, and the new Divisions had shown the courage and discipline of veterans. A hundred captured documents showed that the German *moral* had been shaken and that the German machine was falling badly out of gear. In normal seasons at least another month of fine weather might be reasonably counted on, and in that month further blows might be struck with cumulative force. In France they spoke of a "Picardy summer" — of fair bright days at the end of autumn when the ground was dry and the air of a crystal clearness. A fortnight of such days would suffice for a crowning achievement.

The hope was destined to fail. The guns were scarcely silent after the great attack of the 26th when the weather broke, and October was one long succession of tempestuous gales and drenching rains.

CHAPTER SIX – THE OCTOBER FIGHTING

To understand the difficulties which untoward weather imposed on the Allied advance, it is necessary to grasp the nature of the fifty square miles of tortured ground which three months' fighting had given them, and over which lay the communications between their firing-line and the rear. From a position like the north end of High Wood almost the whole British battleground on a clear day was visible to the eve. To reach the place from the old Allied front line some four miles of bad roads had to be traversed. They would have been bad roads in a moorland parish, where they suffered only the transit of the infrequent carrier's cart, for, at the best, they were mere country tracks, casually engineered, and with no solid foundation. But here they had to support such a traffic as the world had scarcely seen before. Not the biggest mining camp or the vastest engineering undertaking had ever produced one tithe of the activity which existed behind each section of the battle line. There were places like Crewe, places like the skirts of Birmingham, places like Aldershot or Salisbury Plain. It has often been pointed out that the immense and complex mechanism of modern armies resembles a series of pyramids which taper to a point as they near the front. Behind are the great general hospitals and convalescent homes; then come the cleaving hospitals; then the main dressing stations; and, last of all, the advanced and regimental dressing stations — where mechanism fails. Behind are the huge transport depots and repairing shops, the daily trains to railhead, the supply columns; and, last, the hand carts to carry the ammunition to the firing line. Behind are the railways and mechanical transport; but at the end a man has only his two legs. Behind are the workshops of the Flying Corps, and the squadron and flight stations; but at the end of the chain is the solitary airplane coasting over the enemy lines and depending upon the skill and nerve of one man. Though all modern science has gone to the making of this war, at the end, in spite of every artificial aid, it becomes elementary, akin in many respects to the days of bows and arrows.

It was true of the whole front, but the Somme battle-ground was peculiar in this, that the area of land where the devices of civilisation broke down was far larger than elsewhere. Elsewhere it was defined more or less by the limits of the enemy's observation and fire. On the Somme it was defined by the previous three months' battle. It was not the German guns which made the trouble on the ground between the Albert-Peronne road and the British firing line. Casual bombardments troubled us little. It was the hostile elements and the unkindly nature of Mother Earth.

The country roads had been rutted out of recognition by endless transport, and, since they never had much of a bottom, the toil of the road-menders had nothing to build upon. New roads were hard to make, for the chalky soil was poor and had been so churned up by shelling and the movement of guns and troops that it had lost all cohesion. Countless shells had burst below the ground — causing everywhere subsidences and cavities. There was no stone in the countryside and little wood, so repairing materials had to be brought from a distance, which still further complicated the problem. To mend a road you must give it a rest, but there was little chance of a rest for any of those poor tortured passages. In all the district there were but two good highways, one running at right angles to our front from Albert to Bapaume, the other parallel to our old front line from Albert to Peronne. These, to begin with, were the best type of *routes nationales* — broad, well-engineered, lined with orderly poplars. By the third month of the battle even these were showing signs of wear, and to travel on either in a motor car was a switchback journey. If the famous highroads declined, what was likely to be the condition of the country lanes which rayed around Contalmaison, Longueval, and Guillemont?

*

Let us take our stand at the northern angle of High Wood. It is only a spectre of a wood, a horrible place of matted tree trunks and crumbling trench lines, full of mementoes of the dead and all the dreadful *débris* of battle. To reach it we have walked across two miles of what once must have been breezy downland, patched with little fields of roots and grain. It is now like a waste brickfield in a decaying suburb, pock-marked with shell-holes, littered with cartridge clips, equipment, fragments of wire and every kind of tin can. Over all the area hangs the curious, acrid, unwholesome smell of burning, an odour which will always recall to every soldier the immediate front of battle.

The air is clear, and we look from the height over a shallow trough towards the low slopes in front of the Transloy road — behind which lies the German fourth line. Our front is some thousands of yards off, close under that hillock which is the famous Butte de Warlencourt. Far on our left is the lift of the Thiepval ridge, and nearer us, hidden by the slope, are the ruins of Martinpuich. Le Sars and Eaucourt l'Abbaye are before us, Flers a little to the right, and beyond it Gueudecourt. On our extreme right rise the slopes of Sailly-Saillisel — one can see the shattered trees lining the Bapaume-Peronne road — and, hidden by the fall of the ground, are Lesboeufs and Morval. Behind us are things like scarred patches on the hillsides. They are the remains of the Bazentin woods and the ominous wood of Delville. The whole confines of the British battle-ground lie open to the eye from the Thiepval ridge in the north to the downs which ring the site of Combles.

Look west, and beyond the dreary country we have crossed rise green downs set with woods untouched by shell — the normal, pleasant land of Picardy. Look east, beyond our front line and the smoke puffs, across the Warlencourt and Gueudecourt ridges, and on the skyline there also appear unbroken woods, and here and there a church spire and the smoke of villages. The German retirement in September had been rapid, and we have reached the fringes of a land as yet little scarred by combat. We are looking at the boundaries of the battlefield. We have pushed the enemy right up to the edge of habitable and undevastated country, but we pay for our success in having behind us a strip of sheer desolation. To-day there are two No Man's lands. One is between the front lines; the other lies between the old enemy front and the front we have won. The second is the bigger problem, for across it must be brought the supplies of a great army. This is a war of motor-transport, and we are doing to-day what the Early Victorians pronounced impossible — running the equivalent of steam engines not on prepared tracks, but on highroads, running them day and night in endless relays. And these highroads are not the decent macadamised ways of England, but roads which would be despised in Sutherland or Connaught.

The problem is hard enough in fine weather; but let the rain come and soak the churned-up soil and the whole land becomes a morass. There is no *pavé*, as in Flanders, to make a firm causeway. Every road becomes a watercourse, and in the hollows the mud is as deep as a man's thighs. An army must be fed, troops must be relieved, guns must be supplied, and so there can be no slackening of the traffic. Off the roads the ground is a squelching bog, dug-outs crumble in, and communication trenches cease to be. In areas like Ypres and Festubert, where the soil is naturally waterlogged, the conditions are worse, but at Ypres and Festubert we have not six miles of sponge, varied by mud torrents, across which all transport must pass.

Weather is a vital condition of success in operations where great armies are concerned, for men and guns cannot fight on air. In modern war it is more urgent than ever, since aerial reconnaissance plays so great a part, and Napoleon's "fifth element," mud, grows in importance with the complexity of the fighting machine. Again, in the semi-static trench warfare, where the same area remains for long the battlefield, the condition of the ground is the first fact to be reckoned with. Once we grasp this, the difficulty of the October campaign, waged in almost continuous rain, will be apparent. But no words can convey an adequate impression of the Somme area after a week's downpour. Its discomforts had to be endured to be understood.

*

The topography of the immediate battle-ground demands a note from the point of view of its tactical peculiarities. The British line at the end of September ran from the Schwaben Redoubt, a thousand yards north of Thiepval, along the ridge to a point northeast of Courcelette; then just in front of Martinpuich, Flers, Gueudecourt, and Lesboeufs to the junction with the French. Morval was now part of the French area. From Thiepval to the northeast of Courcelette the line was for the most part on the crest of the ridge; it then bent southward and followed generally the foot of the eastern slopes. But a special topographical feature complicated the position. Before our front a shallow depression ran northwest from north of Sailly-Saillisel to about two thousand yards south of Bapaume, where it turned westward and joined the glen of the Ancre at Miraumont. From the main Thiepval-Morval ridge a series of long spurs descended into this valley, of which two were of special importance. One was the hammer-headed spur immediately west of Flers, at the western end of which stood the tumulus called the Butte de Warlencourt. The other was a spur which, lying across the main trend of the ground, ran north from Morval to Thilloy, passing a thousand yards to the east of Gueudecourt. Behind these spurs lay the German fourth position. It was in the main a position on reverse slopes, and so screened from immediate observation, though our command of the higher ground gave us a view of its hinterland. Our own possession of the heights, great though its advantages were, had certain drawbacks, for it meant that our communications had to make the descent of the reverse slopes and were thus exposed to some extent to the enemy's observation and long-range fire.

The next advance of the British Army had, therefore, two distinct objectives. The first — the task of the Fourth Army — was to carry the two spurs and so get within assaulting distance of the German fourth line. Even if the grand assault should be postponed, the possession of the spurs would greatly relieve our situation by giving us cover for our advanced gun positions and a certain shelter for the bringing up of supplies. It should be remembered that the spurs were not part of the German main front. They were held by the enemy as intermediate positions, and very strongly held — every advantage being taken of sunken roads, buildings, and the undulating nature of the country. They represented for the fourth German line what Contalmaison had represented for the second; till they were carried no general assault on the main front could be undertaken. The second task — that of the Fifth Army — was to master the whole of the high ground on the Thiepval ridge, so as to get direct observation into the Ancre glen and over the uplands north and northeast of it.

*

The expected fine weather of October did not come. On the contrary, the month provided a record in wet, spells of drenching rain being varied by dull, misty days, so that the sodden land had no chance of drying. The carrying of the spurs — meant as a preliminary step to a general attack — proved an operation so full of difficulties that it occupied all our efforts during the month, and with it all was not completed. The story of these weeks is one of minor operations — local actions with strictly limited objectives undertaken by only a few battalions. In the face of every conceivable difficulty we moved gradually up the intervening slopes.

At first there was a certain briskness in our movement. From Flers northwestward in front of Eaucourt l'Abbaye and Le Sars ran a very strong trench system, which we called the Flers line, and which was virtually a switch connecting the old German third line with the intermediate positions in front of the spurs. The capture of Flers gave us the southeastern part of the line, and the last days of September and the first of October were occupied in winning the remainder of it. On September 29th elements of a Northumbrian Division carried the farm of Destremont — some four hundred yards southwest of Le Sars and just north of the Albert-Bapaume road. On the afternoon of October 1st we advanced on a front of 3,000 yards, taking the Flers line north of Destremont, while a London Territorial Division — the same which had taken High Wood — occupied the buildings of the old abbey of Eaucourt less than a mile southeast of Le Sars village. Here for several days remnants of the 6th Bavarian Division made a stout resistance. On the morning of October 2nd the enemy had regained a footing in the abbey, and during the whole of the next day and night the battle fluctuated. It was not till the morning of the 4th that we finally cleared the place, and on October 6th the Londoners won the mill northwest of it.

On the afternoon of October 7th — a day of cloud and strong winds, but free from rain — we attacked on a broader front, while the French on our right moved against the key position of Sailly-Saillisel. After a heavy struggle a Division of the New Army captured Le Sars and won positions to the east and west of it, while our line was considerably advanced between Gueudecourt and Lesboeufs.

From that date for a month on we struggled up the slopes, gaining ground, but never winning the crests. The enemy now followed a new practice. He had his machine-guns well back in prepared positions and caught our attack with their long-range fire. To chronicle in detail these indeterminate actions would be a laborious task and would demand for its elucidation a map on the largest scale. We wrestled for odd lengths of fantastically named trenches which were often three feet deep in water. It was no light job to get out over the slimy parapets, and the bringing up of supplies and the evacuation of the wounded placed a terrible burden on our strength. Under conditions of such grievous discomfort an attack on a comprehensive scale was out of the question, the more when we remember the condition of the area behind our lines. At one moment it seemed as if the Butte had been won. On November 5th we were over it and holding positions on the eastern side, but that night a counter-attack by fresh troops of the 4th

Guard Division — who had just come up — forced us to fall back. This was the one successful enemy counter-stroke in this stage of the battle. For the most part they were too weak, if delivered promptly; and when they came later in strength they were broken up by our guns.

The struggle of these days deserves to rank high in the records of British hardihood. The fighting had not the swift pace and the brilliant successes of the September battles. Our men had to fight for minor objectives, and such a task lacks the impetus and exhilaration of a great combined assault. On many occasions the battle resolved itself into isolated struggles, a handful of men in a mud-hole holding out and consolidating their ground till their post was linked up with our main front. Rain, cold, slow reliefs, the absence of hot food, and sometimes of any food at all, made these episodes a severe test of endurance and devotion. During this period the enemy, amazed at his good fortune, inasmuch as the weather had crippled our advance, fell into a flamboyant mood and represented the result as a triumph of the fighting quality of his own troops. From day to day he announced a series of desperate British assaults invariably repulsed with heavy losses. He spoke of British Corps and Divisions advancing in massed formation, when, at the most, it had been an affair of a few battalions. Often he announced an attack on a day and in a locality where nothing whatever had happened. It is worth remembering that, except for the highly successful action of October 21st, which we shall presently record, there was no British attack during the month on anything like a large scale, and that the various minor actions, so far from costing us high, were among the most economical of the campaign.

*

Our second task, in which we brilliantly succeeded, was to master completely the Thiepval ridge. By the end of September the strong redoubts northeast of the village — called Stuff and Zollern — were in our hands, and on the 28th of that month we had carried all Schwaben Redoubt except the northwest corner. It was Schwaben Redoubt to which the heroic advance of the Ulster Division had penetrated on the first day of the battle; but next day the advanced posts had been drawn in, and three months had elapsed before we again entered it. It was now a very different place from July 1st. Our guns had pounded it out of recognition;

but it remained — from its situation — the pivot of the whole German line on the heights. Thence the trenches called Stuff and Regina ran east for some 5,000 yards to a point northeast of Courcelette. These trenches, representing many of the dominating points of the ridge south of the Ancre, were defended by the enemy with the most admirable tenacity. Between September 30th and October 20th, while we were battling for the last corner of the Schwaben, he delivered not less than eleven counter-attacks against our front in that neighbourhood, counter-attacks which in every case were repulsed with heavy losses. His front was held by the 26th Reserve Division and by Marines of the Naval Division, who had been brought down from the Yser, and who gave a better account of themselves than their previous record had led us to expect, A captured German regimental Order, dated October 20th, emphasised the necessity of regaining the Schwaben Redoubt. "Men are to be informed by their immediate superiors that this attack is not merely a matter of re-taking a trench because it was formerly in German possession, but that the recapture of an extremely important point is involved. If the enemy remains on the ridge he can blow our artillery in the Anere Valley to pieces, and the protection of the infantry will then be destroyed."

From October 20th to 23rd there came a short spell of fine weather. There was frost at night, a strong easterly wind dried the ground, and the air conditions were perfect for observation. The enemy was quick to take advantage of the change, and early on the morning of Saturday, October 21st, delivered that attack upon Schwaben Redoubt, for which the Order quoted above was a preparation.

The attack was made in strength and at all points but two was repulsed by our fire before reaching our lines. At two points the Germans entered our trenches, but were promptly driven out, leaving many dead in front of our position, and five officers and seventy-nine other ranks prisoners in our hands.

This counter-stroke came opportunely for us, for it enabled us to catch the enemy on the rebound. We struck shortly after noon, attacking against the whole length of the Regina trench, with troops of the New Army on our left and centre and the Canadians on our right. The attack was completely successful, for the enemy, disorganised by his failure of the morning, was in no condition for prolonged resistance. We attained all our objectives, taking the whole of Stuff and Regina trenches, pushing out advanced posts well to the north and northeast of Schwaben Redoubt, and establishing our position on the crown of the ridge between the Upper Ancre and Courcelette. In the course of the day we took nearly 1,100 prisoners at the expense of less than 1,200 casualties, many of which were extremely slight. The whole course of the battle showed no more workmanlike performance.

There still remained one small section of the ridge where our position was unsatisfactory. This was at the extreme eastern end of Regina trench, just west of the Bapaume road. Its capture was achieved on the night of November 10th, when we carried it on a front of 1,000 yards. This rounded off our gains and allowed us to dominate the upper valley of the Ancre and the uplands beyond it behind the unbroken German first line from Beaumont Hamel to Serre.

Meantime, during the month, the French armies on our right had been moving forward. At the end of September they had penetrated into St. Pierre Vaast Wood, whose labyrinthine depths extended east of Rancourt and south of Saillisel. The British gains of September 26th filled the whole French nation with enthusiasm, and General Joffre and Sir Douglas Haig exchanged the warmest greetings. The immediate object of the forces under Foch was to co-operate with the British advance by taking the height of Sailly-Saillisel, and so work round Mont St. Quentin, the main defence of Peronne on the north. On October 4th they carried the German intermediate line between Morval and St. Pierre Vaast Wood, and on October 8th — in a splendid movement — they swept up the Sailly-Saillisel slopes and won the Bapaume-Peronne road to a point 200 yards from its northern entry into the village. On October 10th Micheler's Tenth Army was in action on a front of three miles, and carried the western outskirts of Ablaincourt and the greater part of the wood northwest of Chaulnes, taking nearly 1,300 prisoners, On the 15th Fayolle pushed east of Bouchavesnes, and on the same day, south of the Somme, Micheler, after beating off a counter-attack, carried a mile and a quarter of the German front west of Belloy, and advanced well to the northeast of Ablaincourt, taking some 1,000 prisoners. This brought the French nearer to the ridge of Villers-Carbonnel, behind which the German batteries played the same part for the southern defence of Peronne as Mont St. Quentin did for the northern.

Next day Sailly-Saillisel was entered and occupied as far as the cross roads, the Saillisel section of the village on the road running eastward being still in German hands. For the next few days the enemy delivered violent counter-attacks from both north and east, using liquid fire, but they failed to oust the garrison, and that part of the village held by the Germans was mercilessly pounded by the French guns. On the 21st the newly-arrived 2nd Bavarian Division made a desperate attack from the southern border of Saillisel and the ridge northeast of St. Pierre Vaast Wood, but failed with many losses. There were other heavy and fruitless counter-strokes south of the Somme in the regions of Biaches and Chaulnes. The month closed with the French holding Sailly but not Saillisel; holding the western skirts of St. Pierre Vaast Wood; and south of the river outflanking Ablaincourt and Chaulnes.

*

The record of the month, though short of expectations, was far from mediocre; and, considering the difficulties of weather, was not less creditable than that of September. The Allies at one point had broken into the German fourth position, while at others they had won positions of assault against it, and the southward extension of the battle-ground had been greatly deepened. They had added another

10,000 prisoners to their roll, bringing the total from July 1st to 1,469 officers and 71,532 other ranks, while they had also taken 173 field guns, 130 heavy pieces, 215 trench mortars, and 988 machine-guns. They had engaged 90 enemy Divisions, of which 26 had been taken out, re-fitted and sent back again — making a total of 116 brought into action. On November 1st the enemy was holding his front with 21 Divisions, so that 95 had been used up and withdrawn. Any calculation of enemy losses during the actual progress of operations must be a very rough estimate, but it may be taken for granted that no German Division was taken out of the line till it had lost at least 5,000 men. This gives a minimum figure for enemy losses during the four months' battle of close on half a million; and it seems certain that the real figure was at least 25 per cent, greater. It must further be noted that, according to the German published returns, 41 per cent, of their casualties were irreplaceable — dead, prisoners, or so badly wounded as to be useless for the remainder of the war — a proportion greatly in excess of that which obtained among the Allies. During the month of October the British casualties were little beyond those of a normal month of trench warfare.

The study of captured documents casts an interesting

light upon the condition of the enemy under the pressure of our attacks. Letters of individual soldiers and the reports of commanding officers alike showed that the strain had been very great. There were constant appeals to troops to hold some point as vital to the whole position, and these points invariably fell into our hands. There were endless complaints of the ruin wrought by our artillery and of the ceaseless activity of our aircraft, and there were many unwilling tributes to the fighting quality of the Allied soldiers. But though indications of weakened enemy *moral* and failure in enemy organisation were frequent, he was still a most formidable antagonist. He had accumulated his best troops and batteries on the Somme front, and was fighting with the stubborn resolution of those who knew that they were facing the final peril, and that they alone stood between their country and defeat.

In the various actions the work of the Allied artillery was extraordinarily efficient. Their barrages brilliantly covered the advance of the infantry; they searched out and silenced enemy batteries; they destroyed great lengths of enemy trenches and countless enemy strongholds; and they kept up a continuous fire behind the enemy's front, interfering with the movement of troops and supplies, and giving him no peace for eight or ten miles behind his line. The "tanks," though only occasionally used, had some remarkable achievements to their credit. On a certain day one got behind the enemy's front, and by itself compelled the surrender of a whole battalion — including the battalion Commander. Much credit was due also to the Transport Service, which faithfully performed its duties under the most trying conditions.

The weather was bad for all, but perhaps it was worst for our aircraft. The strong southwesterly gales greatly increased the complexity of their task, since our machines were drifted far behind the enemy's front and compelled to return against a head-wind, which made their progress slow and thereby exposed them to fire, and, in the case of a damaged engine, forbade a glide into safety. Yet, in spite of adverse conditions, they showed in the highest degree the spirit of the offensive. They patrolled regularly far behind the enemy lines, and fought many battles in the air with hostile machines, and many with enemy troops on the ground. They did much valuable reconnaissance, and repeatedly attacked with success enemy lines of communication, ammunition dumps, billets, and depots. Toward the latter part of October the German machines were more in evidence, but we dealt satisfactorily with this increased activity. Captured German documents bore constant witness to our superiority in this arm. One Corps report described our work as "surprisingly brilliant." Another, emanating from an Army Headquarters, suggested methods of re-organisation whereby it was hoped that it would be possible "to contest *at least for some hours* the supremacy of the enemy in the air." As an instance of the audacity of out aviators we might quote the case of one pilot who, encountering a formation of ten hostile machines, attacked them single-handed and dispersed them far behind their own front.

We inflicted many losses on the foe, but we did not go scathless ourselves. The curt announcement in the *communiqués*—"One of our machines has not returned" — covered many a tale of bravery and misfortune. About half the missing came down in enemy territory and were made prisoners; the others perished in battle in the air, shot by machine or antiaircraft gun, or dashed to earth by a crippled airplane. In a flight over the German lines on November 4th there died one of the most gallant figures of our day, conspicuous even in the universal heroism of his service. Lord Lucas, whom Oxford of twenty years ago knew as "Bron Herbert," had joined the Flying Corps at the age of forty. He had lost a leg in the South African War; he had had a distinguished political career, culminating in a seat in the Cabinet as President of the Board of Agriculture; he had great possessions and a thousand ties to ease; if ever man might have found his reasonable duty in a less perilous sphere it was he. But after the formation of the Coalition Government in May, 1915, he went straight into training for his pilot's certificate, and soon proved himself an exceptionally bold and skilful aviator. He did good work in Egypt, whence he returned in the spring of 1916, and after a few months spent in instructing recruits at home he came out to France in the early autumn. He was one who retained in all his many activities the adventurous zest and the strange endearing simplicity of a boy. With his genius for happiness the world in which he dwelt could never be a common place. In the air he found the pure exultant joy of living which he had always sought, and he passed out of life like some hero of romance, with his ardour undimmed and his dream untarnished.

CHAPTER SEVEN –
THE BATTLE OF THE ANCRE

On November 9th the weather improved. The wind swung round to the north and the rain ceased, but owing to the season of the year the ground was slow to dry, and in the area of the Fourth Army the roads were still past praying for. Presently frost came and a powder of snow, and then once more the rain. But in the few days of comparatively good conditions the British Commander-in-Chief brought the battle to a fourth stage and won a conspicuous victory.

On the first day of July, as we have seen, our attack failed on the eight miles between Gommecourt and Thiepval. For four months we drove far into the heart of the German defences further south, but the stubborn enemy front before Beaumont Hamel and Serre remained untried. The position was immensely strong, and its holders — not without reason — believed it to be impregnable. All the slopes were tunnelled deep with old catacombs — many of them made originally as hiding-places in the French Wars of Religion — and these had been linked up by passages to constitute a subterranean city, where whole battalions could be assembled. There were endless redoubts and strong points armed with machine-guns, as we knew to our cost in July, and the wire entanglements were on a scale which has probably never been paralleled. Looked at from our first line they resembled a solid wall of red rust. Very strong, too, were the sides of the Ancre, should we seek to force a passage that way, and the hamlets of Beaucourt and St. Pierre Divion, one on each bank, were fortresses of the Beaumont Hamel stamp. From Gommecourt to the Thiepval ridge the enemy positions were the old first line ones, prepared during two years of leisure, and not the improvised defences on which they had been thrown back between Thiepval and Chaulnes.

At the beginning of November the area of the Allied pressure was over thirty miles, but we had never lost sight of the necessity of widening the breach. It was desirable, with a view to the winter warfare, that the enemy should be driven out of his prepared defences on the broadest front possible. The scheme of an assault upon the Serre-Ancre line might seem a desperate one so late in the season, but we had learned much since July 1st, and as compared with that date we had now certain real advantages. In the first place our whole tactical use of artillery had undergone a change. Our creeping barrage, moving in front of advancing infantry, protected them to a great extent from the machine-gun fusillade from parapets and shell-holes which had been our undoing in the earlier battle, and assisted them in keeping direction. In the second place our possession of the whole Thiepval ridge seriously outflanked the German front north of the Ancre. In the dips of the high ground behind Serre and Beaumont Hamel their batteries had been skilfully emplaced in the beginning of July, and they had been able to devote their whole energy to the attack coming from the west. But now they were facing southward and operating against our lines on the Thiepval ridge, and we commanded them to some extent by possessing the higher ground and the better observation. If, therefore, we should attack again from the west, supported also by our artillery fire from the south, the enemy guns would be fighting on two fronts. The German position in July had been a straight line; it was now a salient.

We had two other assets for a November assault. The slow progress of the Fourth Army during October had led the enemy to conclude that our offensive had ceased for the winter. Drawing a natural deduction from the condition of the country, he argued that an attack on a grand scale was physically impossible, especially an attack upon a fortress which had defied our efforts when we advanced with fresh troops and unwearied impetus in the height of summer. Again, the area from Thiepval northward did not suffer from transport difficulties in the same degree as the southern terrain. Since we would be advancing from what was virtually our old front line, we would escape the problem of crossing five or six miles of shell-torn ground by roads ploughed up and broken from four months' traffic.

It is necessary to grasp the topographical features of the new battle-ground. From north of Schwaben Redoubt our front curved sharply to the northwest, crossing the Ancre five hundred yards south of the hamlet of St. Pierre Divion, and extending northward along the foot of the slopes on which lay the villages of Beaumont Hamel and Serre. From the high ground northwest of the Ancre several clearly marked spurs descend to the upper valley of that stream. The chief is a long ridge with Serre at its western extremity, the village of Puisieux on the north, Beaucourt sur

Ancre on the south, and Miraumont at the eastern end. South of this there is another feature running from a point a thousand yards north of Beaumont Hamel to the village of Beaucourt. This latter spur has on its southwest side a shallow depression up which runs the Beaucourt-Beaumont Hamel road, and it is defined on the northeast by the Beaucourt-Serre road. All the right bank of the Ancre is thus a country of slopes and pockets. On the left bank there is a stretch of flattish ground under the Thiepval ridge extending up the valley past St. Pierre Divion to Grandcourt.

On Sunday, November 12th, Sir Hubert Gough's Fifth Army held the area from Gommecourt in the north to the Albert-Bapaume road. Opposite Serre and extending south to a point just north of Beaumont Hamel lay two Divisions of the old Regulars, now much changed in composition, but containing battalions that had been through the whole campaign since Mons. In front of Beaumont Hamel was a Highland Territorial Division. They had been more than eighteen months in France, and at the end of July and the beginning of August had spent seventeen days in the line at High Wood. On their right, from a point just south of the famous Y Ravine to the Ancre, lay the Naval Division, which had had a long record of fighting from Antwerp to Gallipoli, but now for the first time took part in an action on the Western front. Across the river lay two Divisions of the New Army. The boundary of the attack on the right was roughly defined by the Thiepval-Grandcourt road.

The British guns began on Sunday a bombardment devoted to the destruction of the enemy's wire and parapets. It went on fiercely during the night, but did not increase to hurricane fire, so that the enemy had no warning of the hour of our attack. In the darkness of the early morning of Monday, November 13th, the fog gathered thick — a cold, raw vapour which wrapped the ground like a garment. It was still black darkness, darker even than the usual moonless winter night, when, at 5.45 a.m., our troops crossed the parapets. The attack had been most carefully planned, but in that dense shroud it was hard for the best trained soldiers to keep direction. On the other hand, the enemy had no warning of our coming till our men were surging over his trenches.

The attack of the British left wing on Serre failed, as it had failed on July 1st. That stronghold, being further removed from the effect of our flanking fire from the Thiepval ridge, presented all the difficulties which had baffled us at the first attempt. South of it and north of Beaumont Hamel we carried the German first position and swept beyond the fortress called the Quadrilateral — which had proved too hard a knot to unravel four months earlier. This gave us the northern part of the under feature which we have already described as running southeast to Beaucourt. Our right wing had a triumphant progress. Almost at once it gained its objectives. St. Pierre Divion fell early in the morning and the Division of the New Army engaged there advanced a mile and took over 1,000 prisoners at a total cost of 450 casualties. By the evening they were holding the Hansa line which runs from the neighbourhood of Stuff Trench on the heights to the banks of the river opposite Beaucourt.

But it was on the doings of the two central Divisions that the fortune of the day depended, and their achievement was so remarkable and presented so many curious features that it is worth telling in some detail. The Highland Territorials — a kilted Division except for their lowland Pioneer battalion — had one of the hardest tasks that had faced troops in the whole battle, a task comparable to the taking of Contalmaison and Guillemont and Delville Wood. They had before them the fortress-village of Beaumont Hamel itself. South of it lay the strong Ridge Redoubt and south again the Y Ravine, whose prongs projected down to the German front line and whose tail ran back towards Station Road south of the Cemetery. This Y Ravine was some eight hundred yards long, and in places thirty feet deep, with overhanging sides. In its precipitous banks were the entrances to the German dug-outs, completely screened from shell-fire and connecting further back by means of tunnels with the great catacombs. Such a position allowed reinforcements to be sent up underground, even though we might be holding all the sides. The four successive German lines were so skilfully linked up subterraneously that they formed virtually a single line, no part of which could be considered to be captured till the whole was taken.

The first assault took the Scots through the German defences on all their front, except just before the ends of the Y Ravine. They advanced on both sides of that gully and carried the third enemy line shortly after daybreak. There was much stern fighting in the honeycombed land, but early in the forenoon they had pushed right through the German main position and were pressing beyond Station Road and the hollow where the village lies towards Munich Trench and their ultimate objective — the Beaucourt-Serre road. The chief fighting of the day centred round Y Ravine. So soon as we had gained the third line on both sides of it our men leaped down the steep sides into the gully. Then followed a desperate struggle — for the entrances to the dug-outs had been obscured by our bombardment, and no man knew from what direction the enemy might appear. About mid-day the eastern part of the ravine was full of our men, but the Germans were in the prongs. Early in the afternoon we delivered a fresh attack from the west and gradually forced the defence to surrender. After that it became a battle of *nettoyeurs*, small parties digging out Germans from underground lairs — for the very strength of his fortifications proved a trap to the enemy once they had been breached. If he failed to prevent our entrance he himself was wholly unable to get out.

The foggy autumn day was full of wild adventures. One Scots officer and two men took prisoner a German Battalion Commander and his Staff, found themselves cut off and the position reversed, and then, as supports came up, once more claimed their captives. A wounded signaller held up a German company in a burrow while he telephoned back for help. Ration stores were captured and muddy Highlanders went about the business of war eating tinned meat with one hand and smoking large cigars. By the evening the whole of Beaumont Hamel was occupied and posts were out as far as Munich Trench, while over 1,400 prisoners and between 50 and 60 machine-guns were the prize of the conquerors. To their eternal honour the Highland Territorials had stormed — by sheer hand-to-hand fighting — one of the strongest German forts on the Western front.

On their right the Naval Division advanced against Beaucourt. On the 1st of July the British trenches had been between five hundred and seven hundred yards from the German front line, leaving too great an extent of No Man's Land to be crossed by the attacking infantry. But before the present action the Naval Division had dug advanced trenches, and now possessed a line of departure not more than two hundred and fifty yards from the enemy. Their first objective was the German support line, the second Station Road — which ran from Beaumont Hamel to the main Albert-Lille Railway — and their third the trench line outside Beaucourt village. The wave of assault carried our men over the first two German lines, and for a moment it looked as if the advance was about to go smoothly forward to its goal. But in the centre of our front of attack, in a communication trench between the second and third German lines and about eight hundred yards from the river bank, was a very strong redoubt manned by machine-guns. This had not been touched by our artillery, and it effectively blocked the centre of our advance, while at the same time flanking fire from the slopes behind Beaumont Hamel checked our left. Various parties got through and reached the German support line and even as far as Station Road. But at about 8.30 the situation, as reviewed by the Divisional Commander, bore an ominous likeness to what had happened to the Ulstermen on July 1st. Isolated detachments had gone forward, but the enemy had manned his reserve trenches behind them, and the formidable redoubt was blocking any general progress.

At this moment there came news of the right battalion. It was commanded by a young New Zealander, Lieut.-Colonel Freyberg, who had done brilliant service in Gallipoli, and had before the war been engaged in many adventurous pursuits. The message announced that his battalion had gone clean through to the third objective, and was now waiting outside Beaucourt village for our barrage to lift in order to take the place. He had led his men along the edge of the river to the Station Road, where he had collected odd parties of other battalions, and at 8.21 had reached Beaucourt Trench — a mile distant from our front of assault. On receipt of this startling news a Territorial battalion was sent up to his support, and all that day a precarious avenue of communication for food and ammunition was kept open along the edge of the stream, under such shelter as the banks afforded. A second attack on the whole front was delivered in the afternoon by the supporting Brigade of the Naval Division, but this, too, was held up by the redoubt, though again a certain number got through and reached Station Road and even the slopes beyond it. It was at this time that seventeen men of the Dublin Fusiliers, accompanied by a priest, performed a singular feat. Far up on the high ground east of Beaumont Hamel they came upon a large party of Germans in dug-outs and compelled their surrender. They marched their four hundred prisoners stolidly back to our line through the enemy barrage and our own.

That night it was resolved to make a great effort to put the redoubt out of action. Two tanks were brought up, one of which succeeded in getting within range, and the garrison of the stronghold hoisted the white flag. The way was now clear for a general advance next morning — to assist in which a Brigade of another Division was brought up in support. Part of the advance lost direction, but the result was to clear the German first position and the ground between Station Road and Beaucourt Trench. At the same time the right battalion — which had been waiting outside Beaucourt for twenty-four hours — carried the place by storm. Its commanding officer, Lieut.-Colonel Freyberg, had been already three times wounded, but that morning he led the charge in person. Though wounded a fourth time most severely, he refused to lay down his command till he had placed posts with perfect military judgment to the east and northeast to prevent a surprise and had given full instructions to his successor. To his brilliant leadership the main achievement of the Naval Division was due. His success is an instructive proof of the value of holding forward positions even though flanks and rear are threatened, if you are dealing with a shaken enemy and have a certainty of supports behind you. Troops who make a bold advance will, if they retire, have achieved nothing and will certainly lose a large proportion of their strength. If they stay where they are they run the risk of being totally destroyed; but, on the other hand, there is a chance of completely turning the scale. For it should be remembered that an isolated detachment, if it has the enemy on its flank and rear, is itself on the flank and rear of the enemy, and the moral effect of its position may be the determining factor in breaking the enemy's resistance.

By the night of Tuesday, November 14th, our total of prisoners on the five-mile front of battle was well over five thousand — the largest captures yet made in the time by any army in the West since the campaign began. And the advance was not yet over. The German counter-attack of the 15th failed to win back any ground. Just east of Beaumont Hamel there was an extensive No Man's Land, for Munich Trench could not be claimed by either side, but in the Beaucourt area we steadily pressed on. On Thursday, the 16th, we pushed east from Beaucourt village along the north bank of the Ancre, establishing posts in the Bois d'Hollande to the northwest of Grandcourt. Frost had set in, and it was possible from the Thiepval Ridge or from the slopes above Hamel to see clearly the whole new battlefield, and even in places to follow the infantry advance — a thing which had not been feasible since the summer fighting. By that day our total of prisoners was over six thousand. On the 17th we again advanced, and on Saturday, the 18th, in a downpour of icy rain the Canadians on the right of the Fifth Army, attacking from Regina Trench, moved far down the slope towards the river, while the centre pushed close to the western skirts of Grandcourt.

It was the last attack, with which we may conclude the second phase of the Battle of the Somme. The weather now closed down like a curtain upon the drama. Though in modern war we may disregard the seasons, the elements take their revenge and armies are forced at a certain stage, whether they will it or not, into that trench warfare, which takes the place of the winter quarters of Marlborough's day. The Battle of the Ancre was a fitting *dénouement* to the great action. It gave us three strongly-fortified villages, and practically the whole of the minor spur which runs from north of Beaumont Hamel to Beaucourt. It extended the breach in the main enemy position by five miles. Our front was now far down the slopes from the Thiepval Ridge and north and west of Grandcourt. We had taken well over seven thousand prisoners and vast quantities of material, including several hundred machine-guns. Our losses had been comparatively slight, while those of the enemy were — on his own admission — severe. Above all, just when he was beginning to argue himself into the belief that the Somme offensive was over we upset all his calculations by an unexpected stroke.

We had opened the old wound and undermined his *moral* by reviving the terrors of the unknown and the unexpected.

CHAPTER EIGHT –
CONCLUSION TO SECOND PHASE

We are still too close to events to attempt an estimate of the Battle of the Somme as a whole. It will be the task of later historians to present it in its true perspective. But one thing is clear. Before July 1st Verdun had been the greatest continuous battle fought in the world's history; but the Somme surpassed it both in numbers of men engaged, in the tactical difficulty of the objectives, and in its importance in the strategical scheme of the campaign. Calculations of the forces employed would for the present be indiscreet, and estimates of casualties untrustworthy, but some idea of its significance may be gathered from the way in which it preoccupied the enemy High Command. It was the fashion in Germany to describe it as a futile attack upon an unshakeable fortress, an attack which might be disregarded by her public opinion while she continued her true business of conquest in the East. But the fact remained that the great bulk of the

German troops — and by far the best of them — were kept congregated in this area. In November Germany had 127 Divisions on the Western front, and no more than 75 in the East. Though Brussilov's attack and von Falkenhayn's Rumanian expedition compelled her to send fresh troops eastward, she did not diminish, but increased, her strength in the West. In June she had 14 Divisions on the Somme; in November she had in line — or just out of it — well over 40.

Let it be freely granted that Germany met the strain in a soldierly fashion. As von Armin's Report showed, she set herself at once to learn the lessons of the battle and revise her methods where revision was needed. She made drastic changes in her High Commands. She endeavoured still further to exploit her already much-exploited manpower; she decreed a *levée en masse*, and combed out — even from vital industries — every man who was capable of taking the field. She swept the young and old into her ranks, and, as was said of Lee's army in its last campaign, she robbed the cradle and the grave. Her effort was magnificent — and it was war. She had created since July 1st some thirty odd new Divisions, formed partly by converting garrison units into field troops and partly by regrouping units from existing formations — taking a regiment away from a four-regiment Division and a battalion from a four-battalion regiment and withdrawing the Jaeger battalions. But these changes, though they increased the number of her units, did not add proportionately to the aggregate of her numerical strength, and we may take 100,000 men as a fair estimate of the total gain in field troops from this readjustment. Moreover, she had to provide artillery and staffs for each of the new Divisions, which involved a heavy strain upon services already taxed to the full. We know that her commissioned classes had been badly depleted. "The shortage," so ran an order of von Hindenburg's in September, "due to our heavy casualties, of experienced, energetic, and well-trained junior officers is sorely felt at the present time."

The Battle of the Somme had, therefore, fulfilled the Allied purpose in taxing to the uttermost the German war machine. It tried the Command, it tried the nation at home, and it tried to the last limit of endurance the men in the line. The place became a name of terror. Though belittled in *communiqués* and rarely mentioned in the Press, it was a word of ill-omen to the whole German people — that "blood-bath" to which many journeyed and from which few returned. Of what avail were easy conquests on the Danube when this deadly cancer in the West was eating into the vitals of the nation? Winter might give a short respite — though the Battle of the Ancre had been fought in winter weather — but spring would come and the evil would grow malignant again. Germany gathered herself for a great effort, marshalling for compulsory war-work the whole male population between seventeen and sixty, sending every man to the trenches who could walk on sound feet, doling out her food supplies on the minimum scale for the support of life, and making desperate efforts with submarine warfare to cripple the enemy's strength. But what if the enemy followed her example? The Allies lagged far behind her in their adoption of drastic remedies, and even so had won to an equality and more than an equality in battle-power. What if they also took the final step? They had shown that they had no thought of peace except at their own dictation. They had willed the end; what if they also willed the ultimate means?

In November, behind the rodomontade of German journalists over Rumanian victories and the stout words of German statesmen, it was easy to discern a profound and abiding anxiety. Let us take two quotations. The *Leipziger Neueste Nachrichten* wrote: "We realise now that England is our real enemy, and that she is prepared to do everything in her power to conquer us. She has gone so far as to introduce compulsory service to attain her aims. Let us recognise her strength of purpose, and take the necessary precautions. It is more than probable that, if lack of war material and supplies does not put a stop to the Battle of the Somme, she will not abandon her plan; on the contrary, she will make use of the winter to accumulate immense reserves of ammunition. There is no doubt as to her having the money necessary, and it would be foolish optimism on our part to imagine that the terrible fighting on the Western front will not start again next spring." And this from the *Berliner Lokalanzeiger*: "We recognise that the whole war to-day is, in the main, a question of labour resources, and England has taken the lead in welding together all such resources. Thanks to her immense achievement in this sphere our most dangerous enemy has arrived at a position in which she is able to set enormous weapons against us. It is the Battle of the Somme above all that teaches us this."

In every great action there is a major purpose — a reasoned and calculated purpose which takes no account of the accidents of fortune. But in most actions there come sudden strokes of luck which turn the scale. For such strokes a General has a right to hope, but on them he dare not build. Marengo, Waterloo, Chancellorsville — most of the great battles of older times — showed these good gifts of destiny. But in the elaborate and mechanical warfare of to-day they come rarely, and in the Battle of the Somme they did not fall to the lot of the British Commander-in-Chief. We did what we set out to do; step by step we drove our way through the German defences; but it was all done by hard and stubborn fighting, without any bounty from capricious fortune. The Germans had claimed that their line was impregnable; we broke it again and again. They had counted on their artillery machine; we crippled and outmatched it. They had decried the fighting stuff of our New Army; we showed that it was more than a match for their Guards and Brandenburgers. All these things we did — soberly and patiently in the British fashion. Our major purpose was attained. We had applied a steady, continuous, and unrelenting pressure to a large section of the German front. It was not the recapture of territory that we sought, but the weakening of the numbers, *matériel*, and *moral* of the enemy.

The fall of winter, with its storms and sodden ground and short days, marked the close of a stage, but not of the battle. Advances might be fewer, the territory gained might be less, but the offensive did not slacken. Still, on a front of nearly forty miles, the Allied pressure was continuously maintained by means of their artillery and other services, and the sapping of the enemy's strength went on without ceasing. The hardships of winter would be felt more acutely by forces which had been outmatched in the long five months' battle. Those who judged of success only by the ground occupied might grow restive during these days of apparent inaction, but the soldier knew that they represented blows struck at the enemy which, in effect, were not less deadly than a spectacular advance. The major purpose was still proceeding.

If you enjoyed *The Battle of the Somme* check out Endeavour Press's e-books here:

www.endeavourpress.com/our-books

For weekly updates on our free and discounted e-books sign up to our newsletter at:

www.endeavourpress.com

Follow us on Twitter and Goodreads.